# Grace

# Grace

## ANSWERING THE DIVINE CALL

A WOMAN OF GOD

Bible references (*Italics*): New Revised Standard Version Updated Edition (NRSVUE) from bible gateway.com

Cover Design: Lovo.Ai Virtual Art
Editing: Chat GPT3.5-4
ISBN: 978-1-7386223-0-6

SEASEM PUBLICATIONS
publications@seasem.org

For You, without whom there would be no Grace.
And for all the Graces in the world
answering the call.

*He will call upon me, and I will answer him.*
Psalm 91:15

# Contents

# Introduction

In a world shrouded by illusions and alluring distractions, a path exists for those who dare to seek a divine love that transcends all expectations. A love that whispers into a person, calling each to a relationship sublime in its purity, abounding in its height and depth, enduring in its eternity.

In every day life, where the veil of heavenly opportunities are obscured by worldly temptations and obligations, this path beckons individuals hungry for elevated meaning and purpose.

For a person with the courage to take such a journey, it becomes one of transformation, a sacred odyssey leading to the very heart of a person's being. There, divine love breathes into the depths of the soul. Its ethereal melody sings through the chambers of the heart, calling the person to turn around and walk the destiny laid out for them. A destiny that grows the seed of divinity gifted them, awakening to blossom into its fullest expression, godliness.

This book guides the reader through the life of Grace who is a witness to the journey of love's splendour towards union with God. Grace unknowingly, unwittingly, then deliberately and resolutely embraces her spiritual awakening, pursuing the nature and offer of the divine call made upon her life towards this deification.

The offer is a promise God makes each person, *You will seek me and find me when you search for me with all your heart.*

Not all perceive this invitation. And not all who discern it, take up the offer.

Through the life of Grace, you are asked to consider the divine call upon your life.

Have you ever felt the stirrings of an invitation, an unspoken drive that resonates within, urging you to explore the depths of your existence, to embrace the fullness of divine love and union?

At the crossroads of destiny, where the soul's purpose and the call from heaven converges, a choice must be made. It is a choice that sets in motion a grand design, an intricately woven tapestry of existence. A plan prepared by God before ever you were born, igniting and illuminating the path ahead when you begin to live it.

This plan leads to the blossoming of your truest self in God's likeness, with the promise of prosperity, hope, and an eternal future, where the energies of God are forever united with your very being.

Grace's story provides the opportunity to witness this living plan in action. Her chronicle is at times difficult to read. Be prepared for the propensity of human nature to err, and to be hurt as the world disrupts, corrupts, and wounds our protagonist.

Moreover, Grace lives in the shadow of a family secret, a truth known only to a few but not by her. This secret infiltrates and shapes Grace's life, fuelling her sense of inadequacy and unworthiness. It drives her need to be liked and loved, and masks all manner of relational self-care and propriety.

By God's grace, it also becomes the fulfilment of all divine promises made to her, though that comes much later in her life.

With unsettled foundations, Grace's moral compass is sometimes skewed by insecurity and fear. She is the sheep that strayed from the good shepherd. But in God's eyes, her lostness makes her the perfect candidate to call home.

As she responds to that call and the divine impetus that leads her, Grace has the sense of being drawn towards something momentous. The path she treads holds revelations both human and heavenly that will guide her deification journey.

Throughout all this, she must learn to disentangle from the pull of patterned behaviours and temptations that threaten to keep her spiritual development limited.

Be emboldened dear reader, for within these pages you will witness the unfolding of a grand design, where truth and healing intertwine with the pursuit of divinity, illuminating the path towards a future brimming with faith and eternal unity.

For our protagonist, this is quite the journey. Grace is not baptised into a religious family or community and must navigate the great mystery via heavenly leadings and the raw materials God gave her.

At first, it is Grace's innate abilities to discern the unseen currents of the world, and to recognise a ministry aiding her that establishes in her a God-seeking spirit. This natural state of clairvoyance enables a person to see everything as it was created. Like many children, from a young age, Grace intuitively sees that which remains unseen by most. This gift that is not something added to a person, is the original design God gave people. Only the world's mark on the heart of humanity prevents people from this natural living. As Grace moves closer to God, as all virtues are turned to righteousness, what is right by God, so too her spiritual sensitivities are elevated into godly giftings drawn into service.

Grace's life trumpets the necessity for each person to be remade if indeed a life aligned with God's will is sought. It heralds the need to become a new person. Born again, of the Spirit. Finding a way out of the maze of worldly agendas, one's own and others', with determination and steadfastness.

The journey is a healing one as much as it is a mystical and soul revealing one—woundedness transformed in and through the glory of God. And as Grace fosters a psychology of expectation and reflection on what is God given, she comes to have faith.

In her quest for truth, and experience of divine love and unity, Grace begins to live by that faith, through which all other worldly endeavours take shape according to the laws of that truth.

Dearest reader, within these pages you will discover that this path is available to you—the pursuit of the truest love that is the unification of yourself with the indwelling Spirit of God.

While Grace's experiences are unique to her, you will recognise semblances of your own journey, and echoes of the call made to you. And there will be moments in this book when you will ask yourself, 'Am I living to God's plan? Have I answered the call?'.

Through Grace's story you are encouraged into a place of self-enquiry and spiritual growth without judgment, to move higher and deeper and more intimately within the heart of your soul's revelation, to bring a new person, a new you, into the world.

Taking ahold of your innate beauty, your unique being, and the truth that resides therein, you are offered a simple yet profoundly transformative testimony to living most preciously your greatest gift—your incarnation into eternal life, divinely unified and whole. And you, dear one, you simply have to say 'Yes', and God will take care of the rest. As Grace witnesses to you, the way is not always clear. And it is not always easy. But *habibi*, darling, I am one to testify, it is worth it!

# 1

## Grace

Nancy Gleeson gazed down at her baby girl. An unexpected pregnancy with an easy birth. Tenderly stroking her daughter's face, she kissed her soft, pink forehead.

'Grace.' She named the little one. 'Our gift from God.'

Grace was born in the late 1960s on Waitangi Day in New Zealand. She emerged into waiting hands without a cry, breathing in and out tiny bubbles.

Cleaned and swaddled, the baby nestled small in her mother's arms. Nancy was joyful. An altogether unique kind of love warmed away tiredness and birthing pain.

Looking into her daughter's wide, unblinking, brown eyes, she smiled, thinking, *You look just like your father.*

Unspoken though it was, that thought echoed into the fabric of Grace's life for five decades before making itself known. For now, it passed unclaimed, a feather on the air.

John Gleeson was absent from the birth. In the army, and trained in munitions, the father-to-be had been ordered to remain in camp on minor exercises by an unsympathetic sergeant. Nancy felt his anticipation with her now. She thought of her parents too, Agnes and Donald Macmillan, who were waiting in the visitors' room.

'Oh they are going to love you.' She whispered into her baby's ear.

And Nancy was right. Three days after the birth, Agnes and Donald took their daughter and granddaughter home with them.

They were smitten. 'Tiny', they affectionately called Grace, their first born and beloved grandchild.

A week later, when John was released for leave, he collected his wife and baby from Auckland and drove them south to Ngāruawāhia where he was stationed. It was there this new family, comprised of two young adults, still in their teens and a four week baby girl, began life together.

In the first two years of Grace's life, the Gleesons moved house six times between army camps in mid-north New Zealand. While it was unsettling for the new family, unable to make steady friendships or establish long-term routines, Grace adapted well to the changes. This was largely due to the consistent, loving presence of her mother.

As each new house became 'home', Grace showed herself to be quite solitary by nature. She spent long hours playing alone. Leaves fascinated her. Farm animals delighted. Dirt was obviously meant to be eaten, and spat out when filled with grit. New people were curiosities and Grace was not shy of them. She had a smattering of words and a friendly manner that endeared her to neighbours and her parents' acquaintances.

And then there was Charlie. Like many young children, Grace had an unseen friend, Charlie, who was the 'bright light' who stood in the alcove with the winter coats. This was in the Makomako camp, a sole house in an isolated munitions dump. Grace could often be found standing in the entrance talking, seemingly by herself.

Nancy was fascinated, convinced there was someone present. Whenever Grace would talk with her invisible friend, the toddler's vocabulary grew beyond the words she and John had taught their daughter. Nancy was certain a very real conversation was happening between Grace and an unseen visitor. John thought it was a toddler's imagination and filed it in his compartment of 'things unexplained and not worth thinking about'.

Nancy and John often saw things differently in life. Together, in their young years, they were a couple of fireballs, furiously hot, quick to burn each other and whoever was in their path. But they laughed just as hard, tried even harder, and would end up staying married for sixty-five years. All their friends and family, even the couple themselves, thought that was quite the marvel.

But here and now, at the beginning of their long life together, the family was being formed. Before moving house, Nancy had learnt that she was three months pregnant. Change was upon them again. As the weeks passed, the mystery of Charlie faded into the background, coming to rest in John and Nancy's memory as preparations for the growing family began. Three would soon become five with baby twins on their way, but not before the Gleesons entered an unexpected season of separation.

2

# Heart and Hearth

A baby boy and girl were to be born into the Gleeson family. With John working full time and unable to care for Grace, the toddler was packed up and driven eight hours north to Agnes' and Donald's house.

Upon arrival, Grace's little brown suitcase was placed in her uncle's room, where a camper bed had been made up for her. She loved spending time with her Uncle Jim, who would lift her high and carry her on his shoulders, eliciting endless giggles.

'It's not ideal,' said Nancy, standing in the doorway to the bedroom, jiggling Grace on her hip.

The room was dull and all three, Nancy, Grace and Agnes, wrinkled their noses up at the fusty smell of a fifteen year old's musty clothes and general odour. Her grandfather popped his head between them, gave a chuckle, rubbed the top of Grace's head and walked back into the lounge room.

Nancy kissed her daughter and set her down on her feet. The toddler ran back into the light of the main rooms.

Agnes linked her arm into her daughter's as they turned away from the room to join the others.

'It'll be fine Nan', she reassured her daughter.

A cup of tea later and with heartfelt kisses, John and Nancy bid their daughter goodbye, promising to return soon with her brand new brother and sister. Grace was filled with excitement at the thought of their return and the new babies. She jumped up and down, clapping her hands.

She held her grandma's hand, waving her parents goodbye as they drove off.

Though the little one felt some concern watching them leave, she was comforted by the proximity of her grandmother and the thought that her mother and father would be back soon.

With their minds at ease, John and Nancy turned their attention to the long journey home and the preparations for the twins' birth.

No one knew then that it would be several months before the family would be reunited.

The first two days with her grandparents were a novelty for Grace. She revelled in exploring the familiar environment and, when finished, would retreat to her favourite spot in the lounge room—a corner nestled between the bay window and her grandfather's chair, with her drawing pencils and colouring books. Grace was comfortable there, though she avoided looking toward the wall length window at the end of the room.

Down the slope of the property, too close, Grace thought, was a thicket of dense dark trees that sacred the little one. Otherwise, she settled in well to this box-size space in the lounge room. She felt safe and secure there, tucked away in her own little world. Unlike the room she shared with her teenage uncle. That room was unfathomable, and situated in the south, it was cloaked in darkness. And after the first night, Grace avoided going to bed on the unfamiliar camp stretcher. It held none of the warmth she was used to and though she didn't have words for the ill feelings that prickled her little body, her resistance to bedtime was persistent. Agnes and Donald were patient with her, eventually carrying a sleeping infant into the room.

Still, the morning brought another day, and the joy of hopping into bed with her grandpa, listening to his favourite songs on the record player while grandma made breakfast, made up for the foreignness of her makeshift bedroom.

It was only on day three when Grace started to look for her mum that she began to feel anxious. There had been no telephone calls and no mention of her parents. As the excitement of staying with her grandparents wore off and the fear of the unfamiliar overcrowded the novelties of treats and new things, Grace began to look for what was safe and known. Her mum and dad.

This morning, after her grandma dressed her, she picked up her teddybear and walked through to the dining room. There she stood on the threshold looking into the kitchen. She cast her eyes past her grandmother at the sink, to the back door. This was the door everyone used to enter and leave the house.

Grace walked the kitchen silently. Agnes was washing the tatties, as the Scots woman called them.

'Granma, where's mummy?'

Agnes turned from the sink, wiping her hands on her floral apron. She bent down to her granddaughter.

'She's getting ready to have your brother and sister remember? You're going to be a big sister, Tiny.'

Grace took a moment to let that register. She did remember. Her grandmother made it sound very special, but Grace was focussed on her mother now.

'Where?'

Agnes smiled at her granddaughter. She loved this little girl so.

'Mummy's at home just now Grace. It takes a wee while to get everything ready for the babies. You'll see her soon.'

'When?'

'Mummy and daddy will come get you when your brother and sister are home sweetheart.'

'When?' Grace insisted.

'Soon sweetheart. Mummy isn't ready yet. You know they love you very much, and they miss you too.'

She gave Grace a kiss on the head. 'It won't be too long darling. Come on.'

Agnes reached into the cupboard, pulling out a piece of shortbread, Grace's favourite. She led the little one into the lounge room and with biscuit on saucer placed it beside her picture books. Grace sat down, appeased for now.

As the days drew on, and there was still no word from her

parents, the small child began to fret. Every day she asked her grandma where her mum and dad were and every day Agnes, struggled to find the right words to ease the little one's concerns.

Still, Grace's yearning continued. At different times during the day or whenever a car could be heard outside, Grace stood in the doorway to the kitchen looking at the back door waiting for her mother and father to come in.

On the sixth day, she watched the outside door longer than any other day while her grandmother busied herself in another room. She heard the shuffling of feet on the outside mat. Running to the door, her heart alight with glee, Grace let out a cry.

'Mummy! Daddy!'

More scuffing of shoes and then the door opened.

'Hello sunshine.'

Mr and Mrs Tremor from across the road entered the kitchen all smiles. They reached for the toddler as Agnes came into the room, but Grace turned and ran back into the lounge room to the sanctuary of her corner by the wall. She plopped down on the carpet and let out a sigh that was part sob.

In that moment, like a small orphaned animal, Grace let go of the expectation that her parents were returning. Time, and the notion of 'soon', slid from her grasp. And the pressure she felt holding onto them, gave way to something else. Pain.

Her little heart broke.

Barely two and a half, Grace internalised in that moment a sense of abandonment and rejection, feeling as if she'd done something wrong to be left behind. It now seemed that her parents and the new babies, her brother and sister were never coming back.

The erroneous seed that was planted by the enemy of life and all that is good, told Grace at this time that she was unlovable and unworthy of her parents' love.

These early experiences shaped her beliefs and future behaviours, leading to difficulties in maintaining trust and forming healthy relationships. And unfortunately for darling Grace, the world gave her compounding experiences that cemented associated beliefs and behaviours. And these became patterns of woundedness.

There and then, Grace didn't comprehend any of this of course. She just felt what she felt, and that was sad.

And though she, like so many young children, was unaware of it, God ensured a heavenly host attended to her with the single remit that sang out, *I will not leave you orphaned.*

A week later and unbeknownst to Grace, another ministry was being poured into keeping her mother alive. Nancy, at just twenty four years of age, had suffered a cardiac event a short time after delivery of the twins. Her heart stopped. By God's mercy, hospital staff at the birth were able to initiate resuscitation until the attending physician restarted her heart using a defibrillator.

It was by no fault of Nancy's that the twins and the family were separated.

She was kept under observation while nursing baby David. While twin, Melody, who had been born underweight was whisked away and placed in an incubator. Mother and daughter were denied touch and tender bonding at this crucial time in the birth and early days of new life.

Restricted to rest and then unable to drive herself the four and a half hours to the hospital, without a licence or the strength if she did have one, and with John away in Makomako camp working, Melody didn't see or hear from her parents in those precious early days and weeks after birth.

Isolated in a sterile chamber without the care, closeness and soothing touch, smell or voice of her mother, Melody's beginnings were alone and detached. This lack of early bonding planted the seeds of a complex relationship between mother and daughter. And while Nancy wrestled with the burden of equal guilt and helplessness, she was unable to be present for baby daughter, and in that era, not expected to be.

It was seven weeks before Nancy and John met their daughter properly for the first time, and were finally able to take her in their arms and hold her. Only then did Melody feel the loving touch of her mum and dad. It was an emotional time when the little one was able to be taken home and reunited with her twin.

Melody grew an independent warrior in life but birth separation had lasting effects on her relationship with her mother, and in love relationships generally.

Only in later years of their lives, when both mother and daughter laid down their claim to hurt and hardship were they eventually able to come together in understanding, forgiveness and love.

Grace's experience of parental separation was different. She had already formed a secure attachment with her mother, but she suffered nonetheless. Feeling abandoned, an insecure attachment formed and contributed some of the main ingredients of her relational woundedness, rejection bias and patterned behaviours that reached for love. Patterns that every wounded child must recognise in adulthood, correct and release for healing, and for a life united with God.

Such was the tumultuous beginning for Nancy and the twins, and for the young Gleeson family.

Agnes and Donald were watching the television when the telephone rang. John gave them the news about Nancy and the twins. They of course were worried, wanting to drive down immediately, but it was decided that minding Grace would be of greater help for the time being. And so little Tiny remained with her grandparents.

Days went by and Grace was none the wiser about her mother's condition. It had been decided not to mention Nancy's health and so no word about her parents or the twins was given.

As two weeks turned into three, and a month went by, Grace settled into the loving care and attention of her grandparents. She no longer asked for her parents. She sat in her highchair, eating her food as part of the Macmillan family. Bedtimes were easier. And there was a general sense of harmony in the house as Grace's sadness and fear surrendered to the stability of Park Road.

While an unseen ministry worked divine energies to settle the child, it was Agnes and Donald who took it upon themselves to do God's work, loving and nurturing her as if she were their own.

Grace became more and more at home with her grandparents and it wasn't long before the little one was speaking with a Scottish accent. The Macmillan's still retained broad accents from their homeland, and each word of Grace's growing vocabulary had a rolling lilt mingled with west coast Glaswegian tones amidst the lowlands sweetness of Aberdeenshire. It was simply adorable.

The little one was content, and though she still called Agnes and Donald 'granma' and 'granpa', the longer they were together, the more Grace related to the older couple as her parents.

So it was an unexpected shock when the Macmillans awoke one morning to find Grace gone from her bedroom.

The day was clear and sunny. Their granddaughter was now almost three years old. And on this crisp morning, she had strode out on her own. Wearing woven trousers and a knitted jumper over a t-shirt, she put on closed shoes that protected against the crisp autumn morning. Her heartbeat tapped out a drummer's rhythm. Blood coursed with determination but her little body was relaxed with purpose.

A tiny hand wrapped around the handle of a brown and battered child-size suitcase she had hastily packed; inside, her favourite brown teddy bear; its left eye recently mended. She held to the case as if she was already a natural traveller. Confidence brimmed with each small step. She was going on an adventure.

A few more paces and Grace would have reached the top of the steep driveway. This was a new thing. The child had never walked beyond the house boundary by herself. Without a gate or barrier to stop her, she had no hesitation, and showed no fear. She moved with a momentum that compelled her forward. A few steps more and she would be out beyond the shire of the familiar into the world.

Suddenly, a voice sliced through her purpose, catching the girl's awareness and halting her steps. Heart and breath leapt out of tune as she turned to see a middle-aged couple walking towards her. The man had a camera in his hand pointing directly at her, and a big smile on his face. The woman looked more serious as she hurried up the incline towards the child.

Grandparents.

Before too long, the little one's vision was entirely taken up by her grandmother's frame.

Heart and breath now no longer orchestrally bound, settled into the regular movement of everyday toddlerhood.

As the older woman spoke, she touched her granddaughter's face and the soft scent of her hand cream enveloped the child. Love washed over Grace. Warm and familiar. She became quite still.

'Where are you going darling?' The woman asked, her concern laced with curiosity.

The child's mind searched her grandmother's face then turned into herself. No longer able to move forward, she looked down at her feet. They were stuck even as she sought an answer.

A sudden panic pierced her. She looked again at her grandmother whose eyebrows were raised but whose voice remained gentle as she lent forward taking the case from the girl.

'Grace?'

Inward searching turned the little one to forgetfulness. Almost instantly, details of her purpose faded. Heart and breath sighed. The call to urgency along with the reason for her plight fled out of reach. The girl's little body shook with inner effort, but it was too late. Shrouded in mist, Grace beseeched her grandmother's clear, blue eyes as if she should know, even as the vision of her mission slipped away from her.

It was then that a truth alive in the recesses of the little one's being floated to the surface. Barely conscious of her answer, she whispered, 'I'm going to him'.

Agnes took her granddaughter by the hand and led her back into the house. She and her husband were careful to hide their amusement from Grace though they did now have the event captured on film. A black and white photograph would forever give testimony to the little one's solo journey.

'What did she say?' Donald asked his wife.

'I'm going to him.'

They both stood silent. Each knew what the other was thinking but neither of them spoke, and certainly not in front of Grace. Donald shook his head. Agnes stroked the little one's hair out of her eyes.

'Come on then Tiny, let's get you a nice milk chocolate,' she said.

Grace readily took up the sweet treat invitation though a small part of her registered frustration in her body. Thwarted. A sort of stamping of feet flickered through her mind but didn't make it down the brainstem to the muscles of her legs. The thought that she was going somewhere important nagged at her, but within the minutes of walking back down the driveway and into the house, it had all but disappeared. And the temptation of milk chocolate vanished any hope of recovering those thoughts.

Grace withdrew to the lounge room where she sat in a corner with paper and pencils. She had been with her grandparents three months now. She loved them and seemed so happy with the daily routines, and had even settled into her camper bed. So, it was particularly strange to the older couple that the toddler had taken off like that this morning.

After telling Grace not to do it again, and satisfied she understood, Agnes sought out Donald who was making a cup of tea.

'Do you think she knows?' She put some cold water in her cup filled with black tea.

'No, it's not possible.'

And that was the only time they discussed the matter. It never again came up in their conversation.

Donald kissed his wife on the lips, and went to sit in his favourite chair to read the paper.

Everything returned to normal. Days went by and another month before John and Nancy were ready to collect their daughter. Agnes and Donald had been preparing themselves. They had created a bond with Grace that would last the fullness of their lives, and it was with sadness that they thought about her leaving.

'Still, it's right', said Agnes to her husband. 'She should be with her parents.'

Donald didn't reply.

So, it was with a great deal of trepidation that Tiny was reintroduced to John and Nancy. She had not heard from her parents in almost four months and had all but forgotten them. So, when they did walk through the door she had watched for so long in the early days of her stay, Grace ran and hid behind the kitchen fridge.

John and Nancy were distressed at their young daughter's fear. Grace had absorbed her sense of abandonment. She had adapted and settled into the new-new, though those early feelings of rejection, of not being worthy or loveable would overshadow divine leadings for many decades to come. And now she stood wedged between wall and fridge protesting that she did not want to see the strangers.

Only after some loving coaxing by her grandfather did Grace emerge to meet her parents. It was not the reunion any of them expected. And, when it was time to leave Park Road, in a most unlike manner, Grace did not go quietly.

Loud tears of protest insisted that she stay. Even the lure of a new brother and sister could not appease the child. Eventually, she was scooped up by her grandfather and placed in the car. With tearful sobs, amidst Agnes and Donald's heart-wrenching attempts to smile and be cheery, the Gleesons left Park Road to start yet another new life, this time with David and Melody, 'the twins', in tow.

These nomadic beginnings set the scene for many moves in the lives of each Gleeson family member. A yearning for security and the love of a warm and united home was indelibly imprinted on them.

And for Grace, it was a long journey to unravel the confusion of heart and hearth longing, to find comfort in the interior place of the heart.

As she found in later years, the conflation of heart and hearth readily muddles relationships. When mind is clear, the way is made for a person's focus to gravitate towards the good that is God, and God's provision. It is then that heart may be healed and the true hearth, the divine home, is sought and found. Prior to that, heart and hearth longing reaches and accepts the mirage of an oasis in other broken people. It takes dedicated attention to unravel early patterns, ensuring the chimney of mind and heart is well swept before seeking home.

At Park Road, toddler Grace set out alone on an adventure. No one knew then what it was she sought in 'going to him', but that act would be a recurring theme in her life—suitcase in hand, travelling the world, inner and outer, to find something, someone—to answer a call.

It is a journey every human being is invited to undertake.

# 3

# Turbulent Transitions

When Grace was eight years old, her father, John made the remarkable decision to emigrate from New Zealand to Australia. It was a spontaneous move that surprised everyone, including Grace's mother Nancy. Not wanting John to regret his decision if she refused to go, Nancy agreed. Additionally, her brother Jim and his family were living in Adelaide, South Australia, providing an added incentive for the move.

McPhail Street had became the Gleesons home in New Zealand. John had finished his army service and the family had finally settled down. They had lived there for five years now. It was where Grace started school, learnt the guitar, and broke her two front teeth after being pushed off a jungle-gym. It was where she learnt to skateboard and where she played marbles with friends for the first time. It was where the older girl first learnt to spell her little sister's name, M E L O D Y, Melody. It's where the family had birthday parties and put up Christmas trees and where Nancy stood on a bauble cutting her foot. McPhail Street was the family home, a few blocks from Agnes and Donald. Yes, they were happy there, but now, the Gleesons were on the move again.

Settling into Australia was challenging for John and Nancy who were now in their late twenties. Their brave decision had little secure foundation at the other end, and the financial transition took some adjustment. At first, the Gleesons lived in a hotel room before they rented a flat just outside of the city. It took a little while before John and Nancy's brother, Jim were able to get their lawn mowing business up and running, but gradually work came and a new life was begun.

Now aged eight and six, the Gleeson children were settling into a new school and neighbourhood. They were navigating new systems, new class groups and peer teasing of their New Zealand accents. But they had each other.

Walking the half hour to and from the Primary School together, the twins waited for their big sister at the end of the day. Grace escorted them home, smiling as they skipped ahead holding hands and singing.

At home, tensions oscillated between Nancy and John who argued frequently while the children walked on egg shells around their father whose explosive temper erupted out of the blue at times.

Grace was certain the increase in volatility between her parents had to do with a secret envelope her father had asked her to hide from her mother. Wanting to please John, Grace placed the letter where he suggested. She didn't know who it was from but her father's words, 'If your mother sees this, she'll kill me,' was enough for Grace to do as she was told and to keep silent.

Tensions increased not long after this secrecy, and from what her mother said in the heat of the moment she had found the letter. And she was furious, hurt and angry. John was defensive while the children were just frightened.

In the night, with her arms over her head trying to block out the shouting, Grace felt responsible. The question of whether she could have done something differently with the envelope and whether that would have had a better outcome followed the child into her sleep and plagued her days, but the answer remained elusive.

In a realm beyond the physical world, a timeless heavenly voice chimed, *Do not let your heart be troubled and do not be afraid.*

But Grace, unable to hear the ineffable, was troubled and afraid.

It was during this turbulent period that she began to exhibit control behaviours. Outside in play, Grace felt an overwhelming need to keep the tennis ball from rolling into the gutter after she threw it against the wall. If she could only achieve this, her parents wouldn't fight that night.

Over and over again, Grace hurled the ball hard against the wall. It sprang into the air, flying over her head, bouncing behind her two, three times, rolling towards the road. With all her might, Grace would dart after it, sometimes diving, sometimes sliding, skinning hands and knees in a desperate act to stop the ball hitting the street gutter.

Her success rate was forgotten and became meaningless one afternoon when her mother gathered the children in the living room and solemnly announced that she and their dad were separating.

Grace felt herself tingle inside. Fear. Excitement. Fear. Guilt. As her mother talked, the nine year old's gaze drifted to the news that was on the television. Elvis Presley was dead. August 16, 1977.

Nancy seemed oblivious. Grace looked at Melody. Her sister was watching the television, crying. David was watching his mum, silent.

Nancy began making promises to the children—new toys, fresh beginnings—a brave attempt to convince herself as much as the children that all would be well.

In that moment, adaptation came to the fore in Grace. With all the change she had already experienced in her young life, she readily switched into family separation mode. No more shouting. No more dread of her father's volatility. No more arguments between her parents. She would miss her dad, but Nancy reassured them they would see him.

Yes, Grace was ready to leave but she remained quiet, not wanting to appear too eager. Melody continued to cry. David stared into space. That was the extent of the conversation.

And then, nothing. No movement. John came home that afternoon. He and Nancy talked. Nancy changed her mind.

Two young adults, both uncertain and barely knowing themselves, made a life-altering decision for them and their three small children. In that moment, they overcame betrayal, guilt, fear and hurt to choose family, and each other. It was a crucial crossroads in the Gleesons' lives. There, on that day, when the world lost a favoured singing artist, and heaven gained Elvis Aaron Presley, something was also laid to rest in the Gleeson household, though undercurrents of tension persisted.

Ripples of broken trust filtered in through cracks created in the marriage that year. The enemy of Love stoked those fires wherever he could so that the young couple would be tried and tested over and over. But what the enemy of God could not account for was the value of family that lived strong and alive in both Nancy and John. The seeds of fidelity planted by both sets of parents, Agnes and Donald, and Martha and Jack, John's parents, grew upright in their children. No matter the circumstance, family kept together.

And so it was that during the sixty-five years they were married, regardless of how many times one or other threatened to leave, Nancy and John always found a way to stay. And, as they aged, the fire in their fight gradually diminished. Later in life, mid-argument they would often simply look at each other and laugh. They knew one other so well.

Now, as mourners all around the world gathered in shock at the death of a rockstar, every angelic being within the heavenly ministry assigned to the Gleeson family heaved a sigh of relief at

John and Nancy's difficult decision and the courage it took for the them to remain united. The error of humanity, and the machinations of the insidious evil one, did not break the couple. It seemed they decided then that nothing would.

Still, the harmony of family life was shattered in these fractal meetings between mother and father, further hindering Grace's relationship development. So too, her relationship with her father seemed strained. At times she wondered if he thought she had betrayed his trust, but too afraid to ask, she remained silent.

During these turbulent times, Grace witnessed the first repercussions of keeping secrets. She saw how it tore at the bond between her mother and father, and how its tendrils sought to destabilise the family unit. The spirit of division had sunk its nasty claws into the couple threatening to rip them apart. And though Nancy and John were stronger than the darkness that came against them, the effect of its attempts left a mark on each family member.

Yes, this was a tumultuous time for the Gleesons but it was also an open door, a chance for God to introduce a new thing into the family. This is when the Light of Glory shines. In the fractured moments, through the brokenness and surrender, when all else feels lost or hopeless, the way is made anew. This is a wonder of God's unconditional love that is all-encompassing, extending to all individuals regardless of perceived worth, achievements, circumstances or experiences. God, who is not in hiding, is ever working for the welfare and eternal life in the divine union of each person. It is there clearly for all to know, when the Creator of everything proclaims over a life, *For I know the plans I have for you...plans for welfare and not for evil, to give you a future and a hope.*

Under what circumstances a person responds to God's call is as varied and unique as is each individual. Some people have an overt sense of mystical leadings or heavenly guidance, while others know this in subtler and less obvious ways. So too, many are oblivious to the divine call upon them. Most certainly, a disruption in routine life for a new thing to be made possible, makes way for awareness of God's presence and guidance.

Grace had yet to understand any of this or to know that her thinking and behaviour patterns were formed through the repetition of childhood experiences and interpretations, shaping her perception and ideas. And, she had no idea how to change that cause and effect eventuation, particularly when so much of it seemed to be put upon her, as is often the way for children in a complicated world.

For Grace, these young years were still setting the scene for her suffering. It would be decades into her adulthood before the God of all grace restored her through the mercy of Jesus Christ. For now, early trials were still being set.

# 4

# 'Go Hug Your Daughter'

The Mortimer Street flats where the Gleesons first lived in Australia, were five upstairs and five downstairs. Theirs was up the top in the left corner and was a bit bigger than most with three instead of two bedrooms. The block was a small community. The children played together and the adults socialised. It wasn't always harmonious between children or adults, but generally everyone got along and looked after each other.

One of the newer residents was a Polish couple with their young boy, Jakub. He was a few years younger than Grace and liberal with his gloating words. Grace was quick to defend herself and the honour she attributed to her family as being the more senior members of the community. So, when Jakub boasted that he was certain his bicycle could beat Grace's new racer, the older girl didn't hesitate to pit her recent birthday gift against his home made creation.

Grace just adored her beautiful new bike. With its banana seat and three speeds, she was certain it would outdo his metal welded, wide-barred, single speed bike. Of course, Grace's legs were a lot longer than the boy's eight-year old reach.

O Brother Pride. As an adult, Grace would shake her head ruefully whenever she had cause to think on this time. Words of a King would ring out in her mind, accurate and apt, *Pride goes before destruction, a haughty spirit before a fall.*

At those times, she would whisper to herself, 'Thank you Father. Thank you for showing me the err of my way through the virtue of your Holy Son. I'm sorry it took so long. Brother Pride, thank you for being the one to invite humbleness, to turn to dust so things of the world could fall away.'

For Grace knew, not as a child, but decades later, that pride entangles a person in the lure of material snares. It places a full-stop after dialogue that has the potential to grow a person. Pride, she later understood from experience, bypasses opportunity that offers spiritual progress.

But sometimes people simply go their own way, and God acquiesces to the human will. As it was when Grace elected to race Jakub. The young girl peddled faster than she ever had, certain of her capacity to beat the boy. Filled with pride in her new bike, a bicycle Jakub's parents could not afford, she pressed forward at great speed.

For his efforts, Jakub kept up most of the way. Only towards the end, in the final thirty metres or so, did Jakub start to tire. True it was that as glorious as the bicycle he had made by hand was, and as clever a creation for such a small child, it was no match for the longer, more agile bicycle Grace was riding. But then, one never knows how such a race will play out. The unexpected is just that, unexpected. And the unpredictable can change the course of not just one outcome, but a series of outcomes that are inextricably interwoven. And what a person makes of these seemingly random occurrences often determines the degree to which the individual remains at a particular stage of spiritual growth or rises to new heights.

On this day, Grace was just about to cross the finish line. She could see the twins and a small group of neighbouring children waving and clapping, cheering her on. Sweat dripped from her forehead as a smile spread across her face. Victory was within grasp. One final push of the peddle and she would win the race.

But Grace did not win the race. And all celebration ceased the moment her bare foot slipped from the rubber peddle and collided with the rapidly spinning spokes of the front wheel.

Nobody heard the angel cry out in warning but the world teetered backwards as Grace screamed.

With the speed and momentum abruptly interrupted as it was, the front wheel locked, flipping the rear end of the bicycle and tossing Grace into the air. She landed partly on the road and pavement, sprawled across the gutter, barely conscious. All thought of competition, dignity and family honour was torn from her mind as pain seared through her leg, threatening to overcome her.

This physical pain was horrendous but Grace would eventually forget it. What had a longer effect was a barb of hurt that ran deeper than the torn wound of her foot. It was a hurt that propped up the growing belief that her father did not love her.

Her bicycle lay discarded and forgotten where it had smashed to a halt metres down the road, narrowly missing the young onlookers. Grace held her blood soaked foot, oblivious to her surroundings. Shock had set in. She became aware of someone screaming. Unable to discern what had happened, she watched the drama play out.

So loud, that screaming, she thought. So loud.

And then the wounded child was scooped up into strong, protective arms. She looked into the face of her rescuer expecting to see her dad. But it was not him. It was a man she called Uncle Darren. He and his wife, Lucy, and their two boys, lived in the large flat downstairs. The two families had become good friends. Upon hearing the child scream, Darren had raced down the stairs of the flats. The same Darren, who was legally blind, who couldn't drive, who used a white cane, and worked for the blind society.

He and John had been talking together in the Gleeson's flat upstairs when Grace began screaming, but it was Darren who ran to the girl's aid. He lifted the limp ten year old up in his arms and held her to his chest, running all the way back up to her flat. No white cane. No fumbling. No handrails. Glory to God.

Darren placed her gently on the side of the bath as Grace's

mother ran water into the tub.

The length of her foot, no longer intact in the casing of skin, which was either missing or hanging from her heel, shimmered with a night sky full of gravel. Adults at once held the girl and cleaned the wound, until raw flesh was exposed. In Grace's mind, the screams then seemed to increase in volume. Someone else was making soothing sounds as the girl stared unblinking at the crimson coloured water. She cried anew as the wound was hastily wrapped before our darling Grace was taken to hospital.

Over the years, Grace replayed that scene, chalking her father's lack of response up to her father's lack of care for her. Grace didn't know that John's time in the army left him deaf to high pitch sounds. She was unaware that he was surprised to see his neighbour race from the room without a word. And she couldn't have seen his discomfort when he realised that another man had rescued his child.

In Grace's eyes, the evidence for her father's disinterest in her was growing. He didn't seem to respond to her the way he did the twins, whether in favour or in punishment. This grew in Grace a feeling of difference, as if she was somehow unclaimed or taboo.

John wasn't an outwardly affectionate man, though he softened over the years. In those days, he rarely showed unsolicited affection to Grace. Rather, he was often prompted by Nancy to move towards his daughter. Grace lost count the number of times her mother said to John, 'Go hug your daughter', 'Give your daughter a kiss goodnight', 'Answer your daughter', 'Your daughter spoke to you John'. It seemed endless. And the look that passed between her parents alluded to something that Grace did not understand.

Nancy's apparent scolding of her husband accompanied by her penetrating stare, and slight nod of head in Grace's direction was enough to move John into action. But he would also skirt around it at times, saying, 'I already did', 'She's just done her hair', 'She doesn't need a hug', 'I heard her'.

This back and forth played out before Grace, who seemed to vanish in their company at those times, as if what occurred was a secret held solely between Nancy and John.

Both parents seemed oblivious to Grace's feelings of awkwardness, embarrassment, and sense of being unloved and unwanted. Perhaps it was Nancy who felt Grace was different and whose efforts to create a bond between father and daughter had the opposite effect of magnifying the distance between them. What would John have been like relating to his daughter without Nancy's interjections? Grace could not know. She only knew that this drama between her parents pushed her towards her father and then pushed her back when rejected. And time after time, episode after episode this layered upon the 'not good enough' feeling that had embedded itself in a little toddler in those early years when she was left with her grandparents.

How insidious the spirit of rejection. How painful it is for angels to watch and to bear witness to the falsities of life's cruelties that the enemy of Love lashes onto people. And O how much harder when it is children who are hurt.

In the short term, our dear Grace was unable to walk for a number of months, reliant upon crutches as her flesh knitted together, skin grew again, and the marvellous nature of the human body healed itself. True, she missed the long awaited school sports day, which had been anticipated all year. As one whose athletic prowess had started to distinguish her and gain her favour among peers, this let down was another blow wrought by Brother Pride.

Yet, it was the longer term effect of believing that her dad hadn’t cared enough for her to come to her aid that fuelled Grace’s suffering.

Yes, this was certainly a season of trial for our young Grace, and it wouldn’t end just yet but by God’s mercy, the Gleeson children would soon receive a gift to lift them all.

# 5

# Seeds of Faith

Faith—*the assurance of things hoped for, the conviction of things not seen.* Elevated out of human endeavours into the biblical world, the Gleeson children would now be invited to taste Christian community in a Bible Club and hear the transformative power of God's love. In the aftermath of John and Nancy's marriage upheaval and Grace's accident, an opportunity arrived to give Grace, David and Melody a new focus and connection with other children.

Nancy and one of the mothers in the neighbourhood attended the same pottery class. Mrs. Williams was a Maori woman, who with her husband and two children had moved to Australia five years previously. He was a builder and she was a kindergarten teacher, both Christian. Mrs Williams ran a Bible Club home group for children once a week and asked Nancy if the Gleesons would like to attend.

Despite their lack of active religious life, Nancy agreed and enrolled her children in the Sunday School. Regarding her own early church life as an important part of her upbringing, Nancy saw value in Grace and the twins exploring Christianity while they socialised with fellow New Zealanders. This also gave she and John some much needed alone time together.

Though Nancy had regularly attended church with her parents as a girl in Scotland, the family had not continued attendance once they migrated to New Zealand. And while John had been a Catholic altar boy, his enlistment saw an end to his church going. Neither Nancy or John maintained an interest in church life. Consequently, none of the Gleeson children were christened or baptised.

Nancy said because she was Church of Scotland and John was Catholic they felt it best if the children decided as adults whether they wanted baptism and in which Church.

So, the Gleesons didn't go to church as a family, and held no Christian practices as such. Prayer wasn't part of the resources the family called on in times of trouble, and there was no daily reference to Jesus, salvation or any notion of victory in God in the family. The inheritance of Jesus was not known, and choices by which to enter God's kingdom were not actively discussed.

This was not because these things were deliberately withheld or condemned. Nancy in particular kept close to her heart her Christian upbringing. When Grace and the twins were small, she regularly read to them from a Bible picture book aimed at teaching young ones the Gospel of Jesus. But as the children got older and the family moved to Australia, with all its challenges, church and God were not a priority for Gleeson family life.

Here now, the Spirit of God in each child was preparing to be nurtured in a season of planting seeds of faith.

In the months ahead, Grace entered hope and conviction, as a small, almost imperceptible grain of mustard seed was watered. As she would come to learn, these early seeds are spiritual scaffolding and support for a person who breaks through into spiritual seeking.

The father of the Bible Club family, Mr Williams met the Gleesons at the door and showed them to the garage where Mrs Williams was organising ten other children in ages ranging from six, the same as the twins, and twelve, a little older than Grace. One of those was the daughter of the house, Tui. She sat next to her brother, Rangi, and smiled at Grace when the Gleesons came in. Grace returned the curtesy. Once everyone was seated, John, who had dropped the children off, waved and said goodbye. He would be back in two hours to collect them. Mr Williams went back into the house, and Mrs Williams sat down, looking around the table with a wide grin.

'Welcome.' She looked at Grace and the twins. 'Everyone, this is Grace, Melody and David.' In unison, all the children said hello.

Grace felt exposed. They didn't know anyone. Tentatively smiling, she thought, Two hours?

Grace could not imagine what they would be doing for that long but for now, she was relieved that it was all very friendly.

'Okay. Let's bow our heads and pray.' Mrs Williams continued.

'What are we supposed to do?' Melody nudged Grace.

'Shh, I'm not sure. Just do what they do.' David, or Davie as he was called, leaned forward to look past his twin to Grace. He nodded okay.

The Gleeson children all watched as each child lowered their chin to their chest and closed their eyes. Grace looked at the twins and with a nod of her head, bid them do the same.

'Lord, we give thanks for our time together tonight as we partake of your Holy Word. We offer a blessing upon each head bowed here this evening, and upon all the families of each child. We welcome Grace, and her brother and sister, David and Melody, who join us. Let them know you tonight Lord. We give thanks for the joy that you bring and the love that we share. In your Son's name, Jesus Christ, Amen.'

All around the table the children echoed, 'Amen'. Grace and her siblings had never spoken that word before. Grace whispered it a fraction after everyone else. Melody and David softly giggled. Grace kicked them under the table.

'You can open your eyes now,' Mrs Williams said. Looking around the table, Grace observed that this was for their benefit.

'Amen' must mean open your eyes, Grace thought.

In front of each child was a book. A 'Bible', they were told. Miss Williams asked the children to open their books at… Grace didn't hear the last instruction. She looked at the twins who seemed just as confused.

'Tommy, show Grace where Luke, Chapter One is please.' Mrs Williams addressed the boy sitting to the left of Grace.

'Yes, Mrs Williams.'

He looked at Grace who slid her Bible, over to him. Tommy confidently flicked through it until he got to the page he was looking for. Grace thanked him and showed the twins where the chapter was in their books.

'Tonight, we are going to read about the birth of Jesus, the Son of God.'

Then, Mrs Williams explained, 'Last week, we read how God sent the Angel Gabriel to Nazareth to tell Mary that she would give birth to Jesus, the Son of God. Tonight we'll read the second chapter of Luke on the birth of Jesus. Grace, would you like to start off.'

Grace was off in her own thoughts about angels. She wasn't sure if Mrs Williams had said angel, but she thought that's what she heard.

Grace wondered if the angel had wings and whether all angels were boys or if there were girl angels too. She caught herself sounding out Gabriel's name, but couldn't quite remember how it was pronounced.

Angels. Grace smiled.

And there, in close proximity but distinctly unseen, a pair of guardian angels smiled fondly at their charge.

'Grace?'

Our dreamer looked up at the sound of her name, aware that all eyes were upon her. David was now giggling openly, until Miss Williams gave him 'a look'.

'Would you like to read the first few verses please?'

Grace's stomach lurched as her throat clamped up. Her voice was already croaky, not due to a common cold as most people assumed but because her vocal chords were fused together instead of resting harmoniously apart.

She cleared her throat and acknowledged Mrs Williams, while her mind recalled her mother's overview of what to expect in the group. Grace was certain there was no mention of having to read aloud.

'In those days a decree went out from Caesar Augustus that all the world should be registered. This was the first registration and was taken while Quir-in-eus, Quirinius, was governor of Syria. All went to their own towns to be registered. Joseph also went from the town of Nazareth in Galilee to Judea, to the city of David called Bethlehem, because he was descended from the house and family of David. He went to be registered with Mary, to whom he was engaged and who was expecting a child. While they were there, the time came for her to deliver her child. And she gave birth to her firstborn son and wrapped him in bands of cloth and laid him in a manger, because there was no place in the guest room.'

'Very good. Thank you, Grace.'

Grace let out an inaudible breath, and reached for the glass of water in front of her. She generally liked reading. Teachers were quick to comment on the advanced grammar and pronunciation skills of the three Gleeson children, which they attributed to New Zealand having better education. But here and now, without knowing the book and in front of so many people, Grace's hands perspired. No one else noticed, and the reading of the Gospel continued despite Grace's nerves.

'Stephan, please continue.'

And so the first half of the evening went through the second chapter of Luke. Grace found herself interested in the story. Melody and David intermittently pinched each other out of view of Mrs Williams, or yawned, and even fell asleep at one point.

Mrs Williams had given a talk after the reading about the significance of Jesus' birth. The Gleeson's didn't follow it as closely as some of the other children, though a number of the younger ones Grace noticed also nodded off. Seeing this, Mrs. Williams took the opportunity to interrupt herself.

'Let's continue this next week shall we? It might be time to have a little break now before we sing.' Mrs Williams nodded to her two children who rose from the table and went into the house.

When Tui and Rangi returned with their father, the noise level in the garage had increased with friendly chatter. It escalated when small faces spied arms full of biscuits, and fruit, different kinds of sliced cake and fairy bread. Grace looked at the twins whose eyes were now wide awake and firmly fixed on the food.

'This looks wonderful Mr Williams.' Mrs Williams said to her husband. Grace briefly wondered why she called him by his surname and not his first name, but this was a fleeting thought, broken suddenly by Tommy next door to her grabbing her hand. She automatically withdrew it. He looked startled. No one else noticed.

'Let us say grace before we begin.' Mrs Williams closed her eyes and took her husband's hand and the hand of the child next to her.

Unfamiliar with the Christian practice of saying thanks before meals, the Gleesons copied those around them who clasped hands with those either side of them. Grace moved her lips, sounding out a 'sorry' to Tommy who tentatively put his hand in her outstretched one. She took Melody's hand who took David's who rather shyly took the red-haired girl's hand next to him.

'Thank you Lord for the blessing on the food, our wondrous light Lord Jesus, for what we are about to receive, we give thanks. May your food nourish and uplift us. Amen.'

The Gleesons all said 'Amen' together with their companions and opened their eyes. Yes, Grace thought, Amen definitely means open your eyes. She had no schooling in the old Hebrew word of affirmation that began or ended a sentence to denote its truth. Neither did she know the Greek translation meaning 'So be it' that punctuated a statement. Grace had not encountered the word 'Amen' in either the Hebrew scriptures or the Gospels, and she had no idea that it would become as familiar to her as the English language itself.

Nancy had raised her children to be polite and to have respectful manners. This was how Agnes and Donald had raised her. With all that sweet food in front of them, it was less good manners and more shyness that caused the Gleeson children to wait to be told they could eat. The other children were polite as well, passing the treats around and offering them to Grace and the twins.

By the end of the night, Grace had enjoyed the stories and the singing, and she and her siblings delighted in the snacks that were not readily available at home; in particular the hundreds and thousands bread, which was usually reserved for birthday parties. Fairy Bread as it was called in Australia. White bread, buttered and cut into triangles were sprinkled with minuscule hard and sweet multi-coloured tiny little balls. Although there were red, blue, green, white, yellow and pink sprinkles, the overall view of the bread was pink. It somehow gave the children a sense of pleasure, a promise of fun to be had with friends. With a mildly crunchy brush of sweetness on a soft cushion of white fluffy bread, it was a young child's delight. To this day, it was the only thing Melody remembered of that time.

Over the weeks, as the children settled into that humble garage, with its leader's generous spirit and the couple's well-meaning encouragement, a sense of joy and ease entered the young Gleesons' hearts. Their faces beamed with the other children, radiating enthusiasm as they all sang the group's theme song, 'Come join our joy time, Bible club, we speak of Jesus and God above.'

And though the children had no framework outside of those

evenings for the culture of Christianity the group promoted, the values inherent in the Bible readings and the shared experience were planted in each child. Grace, Melody and David all received the same seed of faith and spirituality from those Bible Club nights; a seed that God used to help develop a relationship with the children, and in Grace, a sense of reverence and devotion for the divine.

Then, as suddenly as it had begun, the Bible Club visits stopped. Sunday School was no more. The Williams had a work opportunity to move that happened quickly. No one was able to take the classes in their place. Grace, Melody and David simply didn't see Mr and Mrs Williams again, and gradually all the boys and girls of their Sunday School faded from their memory.

What could have been a community building fellowship that the children might grow their spirituality and faith in, was cut short. Friendships and budding companions fell away at the hand of the world's shifting sands, growing in our girl another sprouting seed, that of the solitary life. The shape of Grace in her divine ascent was forming its foundations.

Still, what was sown in Grace in the Bible Club built upon the Bible stories her mother had read to the children. With every attendance at the club, Grace's soul, alive in the luminosity of the Spirit, had generated feelings of familiarity and warmth in the presence of the Gospel. Why? Because *faith comes from what is heard, and what is heard comes through the word of Christ.* Now with the seeds of the Gospel alive in her, faith and hope planted,

Grace was ready for the next of God's offerings in her young spiritual life—Church.

# 6

# The Bubble of Warmth

Grace quietly celebrated that her dad had been an altar boy in the Catholic Church and that one of his uncles, James, was a Catholic priest. Though John rarely spoke about his childhood and Grace had never met her great uncle, she had the sense that she would have liked him. Even then, though she had no language or understanding for the feelings, and didn't really know Jesus, Grace felt that she and Uncle James would have recognised one another as kin; kin in Christ.

It was not long after the Bible Club with Mrs Williams ended that Grace began going to church. Gail Wilson, who had recently come to live in the flat below the Gleesons was a practising Christian. A nurse and a Protestant, she went to the Uniting Scots Church on the corner of King William and Pultney Streets in Adelaide every Sunday evening. So when the opportunity availed itself, now ten year old Grace asked her mother if she could join Gail. Both Nancy and Gail agreed.

For Grace, everything was made right in the world on those evenings. She delighted in being out of the family home with a feeling of grown-up freedom. As she climbed the bus steps and bought her ticket, Grace forgot the world she left behind. Not a thought came to her about what might be happening in the flat between her parents and the twins. Grace was free.

She felt that freedom in the aliveness of her body. As if muscles perked up and nudged one another. 'Relax. Be at peace.' And a voice unheard whispered, *Come to me, all you who are weary and burdened, and I will give you rest.* And she did relax and feel at peace.

Grace's whole being hummed with delight, nodding at the driver, sitting next to Gail, looking at the people on the bus. Though several looked a bit scary at times, they all seemed caught up in their own inner worlds. Old and young, and in-between, all heading to some place.

Everyone moves all the time, Grace thought. She noticed how the world was in motion and wondered at how difficult it must be for people to keep up with it. The whole thought filled her with the promise of new things. Of things different to how they were in her everyday life.

The lights of the city were like stars in the sky, only on the ground and within reach. And the church itself was so vibrant and colourful. Grace was captivated. She felt a sense of 'more' in the world; more that was unseen but tangible in the silence. More that people organised around, shared in, seemed kind and respectful of one another in. More that was also private and individually experienced. It appeared to this girl that everyone under that roof of the church was united in a common understanding. A common good. And as scripture says, *For where two or three gather in my name, there am I with them.*

People showered one another with polite affection as they gathered around to hear the man in the centre of the room. '*Joy*' was the only word Grace could find to describe her initial church experience. The joy that people sung about, knelt with, stood with, clasped their hands together in, though this joy was quiet, reserved, respectful in its solemnity at times. It was like nothing Grace had witnessed. Reverential joy. She was at once caught up in it, curious, cascading inside with the wonder of it, wanting to be utterly immersed in this new life. And that was before she had experienced 'the bubble of warmth' that was God.

Sitting on the end of the pew, towards the back of the hall, Grace had a clear view of the priest. She liked how he came down from the tall wooden platform where the evening began and would stand in the middle of the aisle facing everyone. Sometimes he would walk up the centre aisle, and though he would never look at her, Grace liked to look upon the features of his face as he spoke to members of the gathering. His words largely flowed over her or passed through her, but they changed the room in a way Grace could not explain. And any person his eyes fell on seemed to be moved. Sometimes they would sit more upright, beaming at the man. Other times they appeared to melt away in his presence. Always, the man's words had an impact on the person. Grace was fascinated.

She knew that being in church felt good. It was strange too as she'd never really been around so many adults in one room. Grace saw one or two small children up the front, but other than that, there were none of her age present. It was an evening service so she suspected that most little ones would be home preparing for bed. Grace privately wondered if she should be there at all.

At that very moment the man's voice rang out, 'Let the little children come to me, and do not hinder them, for the kingdom of heaven belongs to such as these,' and her concern disappeared before it took root.

Being in church felt better than anything she had experienced at home or at school. Everything was pleasant. It felt safe, as if she was enclosed in a bubble of warmth. Sometimes, in that bubble there was no sound, not even the minister's voice. There was a sense of wonder and the sensation of being held. It was a beautiful, palpable feeling of resting in caring company; not so much of people but of something present in that cocoon of warmth. Something personal.

True, Grace felt somewhat awkward not knowing the songs, which she later learnt were hymns written for God; they were nothing like the old Bible Club songs they sang in the garage with Mrs Williams. Still, she was pleased to be wearing her best clothes, which seemed in line with other people's formal dress.

At this time in her life, only two years in Australia, Grace welcomed fitting in. Her New Zealand accent had brought teasing from the children at school so at least her clothes looked right, Grace thought.

Nevertheless, Grace did feel different to the people there, as if she was an observer or a visitor in a family gathering. She felt welcome to attend but not quite family.

It seemed to Grace that Gail felt outside of the group too. Perhaps it was because of this or the evening bus times that they never stayed afterwards for the social aspect of the evening.

Grace was quietly disappointed at the end of the night. She liked the look of the biscuits and the glee upon the faces of women and men as they shook hands or embraced in conversation.

As soon as the central man stopped talking, the piano ceased being played and everyone stopped singing, Gail would nudge Grace and point with her eyes to the door. This was the signal that it was time for them to leave. And so it was that as delicately as they would enter, the two would quietly exit amidst a growing throng of chatter.

Grace didn't mind too much leaving it all behind. She felt the joy that had settled peaceably within her might be disrupted by the talk or politenesses of society. She wondered if Gail felt the same. This was a joy that did not seek approval and was not tinged with fear of lack of acceptance. That joy was not reliant upon receiving a treat or having friends and family around her. It was a joy that arose out of the still, quiet peace of that bubble of warmth.

Grace did not question where that warmth came from. She had no words for theology or for God. She only knew that entering into space with those people, and the man in the black whose speech caused the white square at his throat to bob up and down when he got excited, filled her with curiosity about the man called Jesus.

It was a liberated joy that she did not speak to anyone about. No one would have recognised it in her but Grace was excited. And this excitement gave her hope. And that hope brought a great peace to her heart. For so it was, that as members of the one body, with the peace of Christ ruling in their hearts, Grace and all those in the church were called to peace.

When Grace was there, no matter what else was going on in her life outside or even in the church itself, Grace sat there in her bubble of warmth, held in a way she had not been held before. She was held just for her. That which held her didn't ask anything of her. It didn't need to be coaxed towards her. There was no condition placed upon it. The warmth simply warmed her.

From the inside out and the outside in, through and through, Grace was suspended in this warmth and unseen care. She did not know how to describe the warmth as God then. Neither could she hear the voice within that ever so tenderly pressed in on the warmth it was generating, that with unbridled love filled its child with the words, *I am here.*

Grace did not know if others were held similarly. She kept her own experiences to herself. She was so wrapt up in her own delight of it that it never occurred to her that others would be sitting in their own bubble of warmth. Her world, even then, was an insular one. Interior. She had no language for that beauty, only feelings.

During the sermon, sometimes even before everyone was seated, the world fell away. Grace's everyday life disappeared in place of a glorious peace. There was no voice, no vision, no sense of a person or personality. Just loving warmth that felt secure and trustworthy.

As the weeks went by, Grace's visits to the Uniting Scots Church became a regular part of her life. With each Sunday evening service, she grew more comfortable in the familiar surroundings and started to participate in the practices of the congregation.

Grace became familiar with the hymns sung during the service, even though she didn't know all the words at first. She found joy in joining her voice with others, creating a collective harmony that filled the church. Sometimes, she would watch the expressions on people's faces as they sang—some fully engrossed, others wearing a peaceful smile—and she sensed that the music carried a special significance for them.

Naturally observant and curious, Grace paid attention to the actions and behaviours of the congregants. She noticed how some people nodded in agreement during the minister's sermons, while others closed their eyes in deep contemplation. Some individuals appeared moved to tears, while others wore expressions of solemnity and reverence. Grace's inquisitive nature prompted her to wonder about the various ways people engaged with their faith and how it impacted their lives.

The church community became more familiar to Grace as well. She recognised friendly faces that would greet Gail and acknowledge the girl's presence with warm smiles. Over time, a few people even approached Grace, extending their hospitality and welcoming her into their conversations. It made her feel accepted and a part of something larger than herself.

Despite their prompt exits, Grace's connection to the church and its rituals deepened. The experience of being in the church continued to bring her a sense of peace, and she found solace in the moments of silence and reflection. The warm bubble that enveloped her during the service became a sanctuary, a space where she felt held and cared for, free from judgment or expectations.

To her dismay, Grace found that however much joy she felt in the church, no matter how snuggled she was in that bubble of warmth, it was not long into her everyday life that the warmth disappeared. Sometimes, it would last all the way home. If she was silent. If Gail was silent. Sometimes, it would burst with the conversation of a person at the bus stop. On very rare occasions, if Grace got home and went straight to bed, she could still feel the faint press of that serenity on her person. Most often though, it all but disappeared. In those moments of fleeting warmth, Grace reached out with a desire, one to extend the feeling of peace, of joy, one to have the bubble of warmth with her always.

And the words of Jesus spoken millennia ago, echoed through time to her, unheard, *I am with you always, to the end of the age.*

Grace's desire to understand more about the source of this warmth and joy intensified. She listened intently to the minister's words, hoping to glean insights that would help her carry the feelings she experienced in the church into her everyday life. She yearned to discover the secrets of that inner serenity and perhaps even spread it to others around her, particularly her family.

Little did Grace know that this innocent move towards understanding would change her budding relationship with the Church and with God.

# 7

# Conflicted Heart

Entry into another dimension of church experience brought great excitement and anticipation for Grace. As she focussed on the words of the preacher, she began to notice the impact they had on people. And on herself. She heard about the man called Jesus. An extraordinary story. She was captivated. What a glorious man.

Much of what was said about his life, Grace did not really understand. But this Jesus seemed to somehow be able to come into people's life and make all the pain they felt go away. She had heard a little bit about this wonder at Sunday School. This was different. There was a seriousness about the priest that Mrs Williams did not share. She was warm in a friendly manner, though Grace always had the impression there was more than one meaning to some of the things she said to her and her siblings. Grace was unaware of baptism and what it meant to be held within the Body of Christ as a Christian. Despite not being baptised, Mrs Williams always welcomed and encouraged the children with her kindness.

While the preacher in this church seemed warm, and smiled, his words were at times harsh. Though he rarely looked her way, Grace began to feel as if she was being told off. She was not sure what she had done wrong, but she felt bad anyway. Not always, and not for the entire sermon; only when the man's voice got louder, his hands thrust downward in a fist and he began to look piercingly at members of the congregation.

The more Grace listened to the minister's words, the more frightened she became. She started to question the truth of the bubble of warmth. It seemed to her so different to the words the man spoke. Now, instead of basking in a trusting joy, the girl became uncomfortable and suspicious of the bubble's motives. Never while she was in the bubble. While it embraced her, there was only peace, but this peace came less and less as a growing inner conflict arose.

Though Grace could not name her feelings, it was discomfort, the kind that makes a person want to retreat. This was confusing for her. The minister spoke about kindness, about Jesus who healed, who loved all of God's children, and a God who was forgiving. Yet he also spoke about a God who should be feared. And he gave examples of God's anger and the terrible things that would happen to people who went against God's will. Grace had a difficult time understanding what it all meant. She knew what it was to feel fear and she wanted no more of it. And the dear one was yet too young in her spirituality to hear the voice of the One who lovingly sought her out.

*For I am the Lord your God who takes hold of your right hand and says to you, Do not fear; I will help you.*

Grace also recognised that the way the minister said she should live was not how she did live or how those she knew lived. Grace had already succumbed to a neighbourly influence of seeing how many sweets each could extract from the local supermarket without paying. For Grace, this was a game, a competition and a way to secure a friendship. Only when she told her mother about it and her mother named it stealing did Grace repent. She never stole another thing in her long life and God's humour saw her later working at the same supermarket for six years.

Well, Grace knew that her family was not as polished as the minister demanded. She knew they drank and swore and argued and fought, and did not go to church. Did this mean that her family was condemned? Would her parents and the twins be taken from her, and thrown into the fiery pit that awaited all sinners? Hell?

Grace's heart was conflicted. Gradually, the hope that had been kindled in this young girl, and the light that had shone for God in her, began to fade.

It was about this time, an ache appeared. Grace did not know it was an old pain from her toddler years, but when it became time for church, her stomach would turn itself into knots of protest. The pain would begin on Saturday evening and last all the way through to Sunday night. No longer was it a joy to sit in church. Grace sat in the pew nursing her sore stomach, trying to hide her pain from Gail.

And as Grace sat there in discomfort, the spirit of division sunk its hooks deeper into the child. And the voice of anxiety grew within her. As a result, Grace started to miss the odd Sunday. She was torn between hope and despair but listening to the minister's words had begun to feel like she was betraying her family. The warm bubble had not come to greet her for weeks, and she feared that it knew. Somehow it knew that she was conflicted. She felt bad about this as well, as if it was her fault the bubble had disappeared. Remnants of her experience of early abandonment by her parents reared up. She could not hear the plea of God within her, *Do not fear, for I am with you; do not be afraid, for I am your God, I will strengthen you; I will help you; I will uphold you with my victorious right hand.*

Grace could not perceive the glorious peace that longed to envelope her. She only heard the minister's words and the myriad feelings that accompanied them. She was afraid that if she continued going to church she would become ashamed of her parents. Ashamed of all of her family, even her grandparents, because though they had been in their youth, they were now not church goers. These were thoughts that tormented the girl.

One evening proved to be the end of Grace's early church discovery. She sat in her usual place next to Gail towards the back of the church. The lady on the piano had finished the opening music. The minister began with great emotion to speak. Grace startled. Ever so sneakily, without her realising it, Grace found herself nodding. And though it was an imperceptible nod, Grace felt real conviction within her that he was right. The minister was right in what he was saying. Grace jolted upright. She practically jumped in her seat. Fear ran through her little body causing her to physically shudder.

No! She exclaimed inside. No. Grace determined then and there that she would close her ears to the words of the minister. And she did right there and then.

Grace resolutely refused to let her family be trapped in that awful place, with fire and nightmares and no hope of ever getting out. That could not happen. And though a part of her wanted to belong to the church and all that was being said, and a deep part of her agreed with the goodness the minister spoke about, the threatening part of the message frightened the child no end.

Her overwhelming compulsion and the greater part of her, sought to protect and remain with her family. Grace could not choose church over them. And she knew with certainty that they would not choose church. So for the second time in her young life, Grace's heart broke.

At ten years old she said goodbye to church, to the bubble of warmth, and to God. A voice most tender called out in the wilderness of Grace's mind, *I am here,* but remained unheard.

At this time in her life, Grace had no friends to talk about this experience with or even words to share with her family. She did not know that it is what can happen when a person comes into the joy of God and there is no foundation or reflection capacity for that joy in the everyday life. Conflict might arise. An adult, under regular circumstances, develops ways of processing inner conflict, and often has ways of airing their concerns. The advent of the internet and artificial intelligence permits young and old to search the internet or discuss with a chatbot any manner of issues, but this was not available for Grace in the 1970s. And, without the ability to work through the myriad of conflicting thoughts and emotions, Grace's meeting of the divine through church was short-lived.

What is more, it opened the already established wound of rejection, and the feeling of not being good enough.

O, how many children are arrested in their spiritual development due to early pains that have found their way into internal beliefs. How those unfortunate beliefs and ideas have a way of robbing a child, a teenager, an adult, of the glory and splendour God lays before them in invitation to enter into sublime relationship with all that is holy.

Our dear Grace was not aware of those threads of early development. How could she be? She was not yet established enough in her relationship with God to discern the difference between God's love and scripture that humans interpret and deliver; interpretation that can at times serve to separate the unique individual from God's love.

Grace ran hard into the challenge for some who discover Christ outside of the Christian family tradition. They look to the Church to reflect the mystical and personal experience of the holy, and of the Trinity, but the Church itself can at times repel rather than invite, affirm, understand and accept. Sadly, this was Grace's experience.

Despite this early sense of rejection, our young one's exposure to church and Sunday School beforehand, introduced Grace to Jesus though she did not yet have a personal relationship with him. Whatever warmth she might have felt towards the man was muddled with the minister's sermons that seemed to condemn her and her loved ones. So she concluded in her rather black and white way that there was not enough evidence to support her initial feelings of comfort, security and warmth associated with the man called Jesus. And she let him go, moving on with her childhood life.

Most fortunately, God had no such ambiguity. Jesus continued to reach for his darling child, and even as she pushed him away he promised her, *I will seek the lost, and I will bring back the strays, and I will bind up the injured, and I will strengthen the weak.*

Jesus was not prepared to lose this member of his flock. That is what God does; he actively seeks out the wandering, the isolated, the sheep that have strayed. And by God's grace, every curious child, every spiritually seeking person is reoriented towards the wonder of creation and the love of God. And this reorientation happens through whatever is available in the world alongside the ministry of angels, saints and celestials working for God in a person's life.

Many years later, Grace would learn this about God. She would understand that there is no need to turn away from God because of the human message in the world. That when a person puts trust in God, all that is needed is to continue living and letting God lead. Everything else is worked out through God's divine ministry.

Grace did not know that as a child. At the time, there seemed only one solution, which was to remove herself from the discomfort. And so, it was not long before she asked her mother if she could stop going to church. When Nancy asked why, Grace had no answer to give her. How could she find words to explain the uneasiness that had robbed her of the great joy she had found in the bubble of warmth that was God.

Though Grace had no words for the inner conflict she felt, it was real, with actual consequences. Set to sea without the spiritual and moral stability of a sail and compass Church can provide, Grace was left navigating the world by the world's standards. Those standards support individualism, secularism, self-coping strategies and law-abiding guidelines that are ill-equipped to nurture and keep safe the innocent seeker, let alone the wounded child as she finds her way in the world.

The impact of this experience on Grace's faith and young life was significant. As we will see in the next chapter, the immediate ramifications left her open to the harshness of the world without the support and covering Church can offer.

# 8

# Innocence Shattered

The following year, when Grace was eleven years old and the twins were nine, John and Nancy moved their family into a rental house a little closer to town. This meant a whole new primary school for the last year of Grace's early school life. Three primary schools in six years. Goodbyes to friends were given with promises of reuniting in high school. This thought eased the parting somewhat for Grace who was excited about starting afresh.

She was pleased to be away from the neighbourhood of Kurralta Park and those flats. Like many developing girls Grace had experienced sexual harassment by one of her friend's older brothers. She was careful to avoid the sixteen year old, Rodney when she visited her friend Naomi. But the girls were not always successful in their timing. Coming home from school expecting Naomi's parents to be there, on more than one occasion they were ambushed by waiting teenage boys in the house. The boys at first threatened the girls, pinched them and made lewd comments. The girls ran out of the house and back to the flats where Grace and her family lived. But on one occasion, when Naomi was sure her brother was away with friends, the sixteen year old had come home early from his camp. The girls didn't hear him or his friend in the boy's room when they entered the house. Naomi's parents were still at work.

It wasn't until the girls started preparing a snack for themselves that the larger boys appeared in the doorway. Grace and Naomi dropped what they were doing and ran. Naomi went for her room while Grace ran down the hallway. She could hear her friend swearing and calling out to her brother to leave them alone. Grace was trapped. Rodney pinned her to the floor.

The more grotesque of human behaviours loomed large already in these teenage boys. Lust. Power over the powerless. Grace fought, kicking and punching and screaming at him, but he was much stronger and simply laughed at her.

A little part of Grace fell into forgetfulness then. She peeled away out of her skin, dissociating from the situation. Ashamed of her weakness, and even of her budding womanhood, as the boy took delight in exploring and assaulting her upper body, a part of Grace died in that hallway.

And the angels present wept.

Grace did not know this behaviour. And she did not know Jesus' healing yet. She was a girl who enjoyed art and sports day and nature. She was quiet, playful, competitive yet honest. When the same friend encouraged Grace and the twins to steal chocolates from the local shops, Grace turned her back on that friendship.

In essence, she was an innocent. Her eyes sparkled with excitement at the world, a flower, a small animal. She marvelled at the vibrant colours of the greens of different grass, her fingers delighting in dew on morning blades. She eagerly shared stories and enjoyed dress ups and play with her brother and sister, her face beaming with pure delight to see the joy this gave the adults.

She played with friends and avoided the habits of smoking they tempted her into. Her innocence shone through unguarded enthusiasm and a genuine love of life. Yes, she had encountered much already in her childhood through the dynamics of her young parents and the disruptions of moving houses, but she had been completely unaware of the cruelties and darker impulses of people in a world that offered so much beauty.

Grace welcomed the shorter walk to the new school, ten minutes instead of an hour, and the lessons seemed considerably easier than her former school. But she made no new friends there and once again encountered the sinful nature of people.

Outside of school, she and a local Indigenous girl, Petra, who didn’t go to school, liked to kick the ball at the local park, just on the corner of the road where Grace lived. Petra’s two brothers sometimes joined in. Grace and the younger brother Ash had a lovely banter between them. They didn't visit each other's houses, but the three of them enjoyed kicking the ball with mock competitions and the occasional meet up at the nearby shop over a video game.

All this changed when the family's older cousin came to live with them. Penny, her name was, and she didn't like Petra playing with a non-Indigenous girl. On one occasion, as Petra and Grace ran around the park, kicking the round ball back and forth, Penny arrived on the scene with three friends. Showing off in front of them, she took the ball up in her hands and started menacing Grace with it.

What manner of trials befall humanity's children that neither adult or authority witness.

Grace ignored the girl, moving to the side of her. Her heart thumped as she turned to leave and quickened her step. Penny was not to be ignored. She lunged at Grace and throwing her cardigan over Grace's face, used her fist to beat into the side of our young girl's head. Some of Penny's family laughed. Others were silent. Petra watched on.

Grace recovered from the shock of the attack. Her head hurt but she kept walking.

Keep going, she told herself. Don't retaliate. That will make it worse. She's too big for you.

Another voice that remained unheard by Grace echoed her inner dialogue.

*Be strong and courageous. Do not be afraid or terrified because of them, for the LORD your God goes with you; he will never leave you nor forsake you.*

Penny dropped behind to the applause of her friends. Grace walked on. She avoided Penny and her family from that day forth, and feeling betrayed by Petra, cut all ties with her.

Grace spent more time at home with the twins after this episode of violence, and when the park was clear of the rougher adolescents, Grace and her sister Melody would play on the swings or closer to the courts in front of the adult tennis club.

On this one day, a boy from their new primary school, who lived on the other side of the park, came up to them. Dennis began menacing Melody. With every word, the child, courageous as she was, gave a word back, until the older boy lunged at her. Grace quickly stepped between them. Melody ducked aside, but Dennis' momentum continued. He pushed Grace, who was a head shorter than him, up against the wall, pinning her wrists above her head.

The pain of her skin grazing on rough brick disappeared as the twelve year old boy attempted to violate her. Despite Grace kicking and struggling, he managed to lift up her dress and fumble for her panties even as his other hand pulled down the zipper on his trousers when something in Grace snapped. Perhaps it triggered the former fear of Rodney's assault. Or maybe it was simply a latent part of herself, but there and then something erupted in Grace.

The girl cried out.

But Grace did not just cry out. Suddenly, she raged. And this rage fuelled a strength she had not known existed in her. A guttural scream rose up in her and it seemed to bring supernatural power that surged up from her feet through her torso so that in one fluid motion her whole body convulsed up and forward.

*The Lord is my strength and my shield.*

She broke free of her prison and pushed the boy so hard, he lifted off the ground and fell back.

Grace had no memory of this happening. She had disappeared. As Grace recalled that time, it was her sister who had been assaulted. It was many years later when she was visiting with Melody that her sister corrected Grace's recollection of the time. As if a key unlocked the memory, it all came back to her.

Dennis had scrambled to his feet and advanced on Grace again. As she pushed herself off the wall, he ran forward and drove his fist into Grace's eye. It bloodied and closed immediately, but the eleven year old did not notice. Something primal in her was alive and fierce now. She let out a fabric-ripping scream that caused the boy to pale and run for his bike. He sped off to escape the creature that now pursued him, but Grace was right behind him. It seemed that her bicycle flew in pursuit. And of this too, she was not aware.

To this day Grace cannot say what would have happened if she had caught up to him. Pure violence ran through her. Violence that was itself in control. Rage so consuming for a child so young.

When these memories were integrated decades later, Grace thanked God that his mercy spared her the repercussions of that rage, and the damage it might have wrought. As it was, Grace was so blinded by her fury that she misjudged a corner turn and her bike wheel buckled beneath the centre bar. She fell just outside the tennis courts. The adults playing stopped what they were doing and came to the fence to see if the girl was all right. Grace did not at first notice. She was yelling after the boy, unintelligible words filled with fury.

Eventually, she sagged. Anger gave way to shock. Shock noticed bodily pain. Pain spoke of grazed wrists, knees, ankles and shins, and an eye that for a reason she could not grasp was blind to her. Pain, brought awareness. Awareness gave way to exhaustion, which ushered in tears.

From somewhere Grace could not see without turning her whole head, voices called out, 'Are you okay? Are you okay?' They sounded so distant; an echo in the air pushing its way into her consciousness.

Hearing the girl's distress more adults had stopped playing and had come to the court fence to check on the child.

Grace realised for the first time that she was on the ground and that they were calling to her.

Embarrassment mingled with shame and defeat. She looked up to see the boy speeding around the corner towards his home, now out of sight.

He got away, Grace registered disappointment.

Bringing her attention back to the onlookers, she replied, 'Yes. Yes. I'm okay'.

Though it took all of her now aching human strength to get up, she made not a sound as she extricated herself from the twisted bike. Straightening it up as best she could, Grace turned her back on those who had come to her aid.

Too late, she unfairly accused, and slowly, painfully, Grace limped home with her twisted bicycle and Melody silently walking beside her.

When Nancy saw the swelling and bruising of Grace's eye she was aghast. Melody told their mother what happened. Not aware of the other injuries, Nancy insisted that Grace march back down to the park with her, and to the boy's house. She pounded on the door. The boy's mother answered.

'Look what your son has done. Just look', Nancy exclaimed.

The mother knew something had happened. Dennis had a scratch on his face when she saw him enter the house out of breath. Apparently, when Grace had pushed him, her fingernail had caught his cheek. He had arrived home out of breath and a little shaken himself, and his mother had questioned him but he had given no reply.

She went and brought Dennis to the door where he was made to apologise. Grace stood there, but she was not present. Her body was sore and tired and she wanted to rest. Her mind had fled somewhere else.

'You're lucky we don't go to the police,' Nancy continued.

'Please. We will take care of it,' the mother attempted to reassure Nancy. 'Nothing like this will happen again.'

'It better not...' Nancy was worked up now. A mother defending her child. 'What if he had succeeded?' She demanded. 'What then? What kind of child are you raising?' Nancy was relentless.

The woman hung her head as she nodded.

Mother and daughter walked home. Grace was quietly proud of her mum.

School proved not as conducive to justice. She hadn't been at the new school long, and had made no new friends. While Dennis was absent from the camp scheduled that week, his closest friend, Timothy was not, and he ensured everyone knew that Grace had been beaten.

Children can indeed be cruel at times. Grace was ostracised for her mother's behaviour, for the fact that the violent boy had been forbidden to go to camp. She was blamed for his absence and punishment. No one played with her, and at night as she tried to sleep, each child took turns at calling out hurtful names to her. Grace lay there attempting to close her ears to their barbs, but tears made wet her pillow as she pretended to sleep.

The girl had been afraid to sleep since the assault, and in the dormitory where she didn't feel safe, the fear and fight of the week past kept playing over in her mind. Her body tremored while her heart raced.

Unbeknownst to Grace, a gentle heavenly hand came to rest upon her head each night, easing her pain, finally allowing her to surrender to a restful slumber.

*Blessed be the God and Father of our Lord Jesus Christ, the Father of mercies and God of all comfort.*

This rest gave her courage to face the next day away from home amongst unfriendly and openly hostile children.

It gave Grace no pleasure, indeed it arose in her such pity, when Melody, all those years later, told her older sister that Dennis had been orphaned not long after the incident.

Less than a year and a half after he attacked Grace, both of Dennis' parents were killed in a car accident. He was put into a foster home. Grace shook her head. She thought of her own parents and grandparents, and could only have sympathy for him.

'How sad,' she said.

Needless to say, these early experiences of violence, and more, left a mark upon Grace. Her innocence was shattered. She did not know it then, and not even in her adulthood, until the second half of her life that Jesus can and has taken that pain upon himself. Through the prayer of the heart, she came to know and feel the truth that Christ really does *heal the brokenhearted and bind up their wounds*.

What's more, all things through him are turned to righteousness so that even these assaults and those unspoken were made good and right through a love she would give him alone. For now, her shaken foundations left the door slightly ajar for the comfort God promises.

# 9

# Hope in a Saviour

In Adelaide, in the 1980s, large buses filled with all manner of books—mobile libraries—serviced the neighbourhoods. These buses would visit the same streets every fortnight, providing access to books for those who couldn't travel to a public library. This was before the internet, smart phones, tablets, Kindle or AI speech readers. One of these mobile libraries stopped in the street of the Gleesons' new home.

Grace's family had moved once more, and now to a longterm government-assisted housing maisonette in a suburb much farther south than their former house. It was a red brick half house, with a central wall shared with the family next door. The house was a lot smaller than the rental they'd come from, but it offered stability and a welcome change of environment.

Grace had now moved house twelve times in her fourteen years, and though she had to catch two buses to high-school, the children enjoyed the adventure of finding their way together.

The mobile library made a stop on Grace's street every two weeks, thanks to Nancy and Melody's avid readership. Grace, more inclined towards sports, drawing, painting, and writing, found herself infrequently visiting the library bus. On the rare occasion that she did go with her mum and sister, she didn't stay long.

True, it was a curious place. It was as if the lives of all the characters popped their heads out and conversed with each other, oblivious to the browsing visitors. It was vibrant with the possibilities and adventures that all the pages offered, but the air was stuffy with people odour and used books smell, and the space was far too cramped and overwhelming for Grace. She was happy to leave the browsing to her mum and sister.

On one occasion, Nancy borrowed a novel for her from the mobile library. Handing it to her daughter, she said, 'It's about Jesus, but it's fiction, a story. I think you'll like it.'

And Nancy was right. The young girl was captivated. It was the first book that had a profound impact on her. For readers, there are generally a few precious books dear to the heart that have greatly influenced their lives. Often, people say that these books have come to them by way of mysterious means or out of the blue, recommended by friends or strangers. Countless stories exist of books seeming to jump off shelves and fall at the feet of their intended reader. In every instance, the content has delivered great personal and spiritual blessing to the person.

What people don't see is the precise ministry that orchestrates these encounters. They are never mere coincidences. Just as when a person unexpectedly meets someone who inspires, uplifts, and guides them, these encounters are part of divine providence. These persons and the books that bring spiritual growth are part of God's carefully laid plans, carried out by unseen servants of grace. It merits people to pause and give thanks for this divine orchestration that leads them closer to God.

And so, on the 8th of May 1982, the angel responsible for Grace's spiritual well-being communicated with the angel in charge of Nancy. Through this divine chain of communication, everything aligned to highlight one small blue book among the shelves of the library bus. As Nancy browsed the rows of publications, her attention was drawn to this seemingly ordinary novel that stood out. Unbeknownst to her, it was the indwelling Spirit of God that generated the warm feeling of peace and quiet joy within her as she took the book in her hands. Thinking of Grace, she decided to borrow it for her daughter.

Nancy believed that this book, with its perfect infusion of spiritual values, would add to the continuity of God in Grace's life. Special books have the power to stretch the reader, challenging them intellectually, emotionally, and spiritually, always guiding them towards eternal values. It is through these eternal values that individuals embark on the pinnacle of life's journey, the journey home to God.

This little gem of a book told a tale reminiscent of Moses' early life and the miracles, healings, and faith associated with Jesus. It was a narrative distant enough from the confines of organised religion that Grace was now shy of, while allowing the teenager to connect with the story's themes of abandonment and longing. She immersed herself in the kind woman's nurturing of the baby found in the rushes, rejoiced in the protagonist's radiant adolescence and solitary adulthood, and marvelled at his equal treatment of all creatures and his ability to command the elements.

Grace's heart resonated deeply with the man. As he wandered the lands, he basked in the changing seasons and knew their propensities, embracing them all as unique and precious.

Grace read how the man walked into a village in the middle of a drought. Where once the tribe had believed in a single God, they now had little faith or hope, such were their hardships. They fought among themselves, had given up on ideas and plans for the future. They were slaves to the weather and their own despair. The man saw their suffering and had compassion. He brought healing to one of the farmer's daughters who had been bedridden with a fever. The village had expected her to die but by his hand, she lived. By his words of encouragement, and the assistance he gave to all, he brought emotional healing to the men who had all but given up. But still, there was great despair among the people.

One night this man went outside while everyone slept. He raised his arms in the air and spoke to the Almighty God and commanded rain. And as the villagers woke and walked outside to see him standing there so too the night sky opened releasing precious and steady streams of water. The drought had broken. Laughter replaced tears.

And they looked upon this man in wonder; he who had brought light into a broken place, mending bodies and hearts, and who now stood responsible for saving crops and filling dry and hungry mouths. Every person in that village was renewed, and made of that renewal right ways in their life.

Grace fell in love with the man. Her heart sang in triumph and in the privacy of a reader. It was as if she knew his innermost being. As a reader and not a character in the book who only saw snippets of the man's life, Grace was privy to everything about him, and she adored that intimacy. She knew the truth of his birth, the upbringing he had, the pains and the losses, the relationship with nature he relished and the solitude he protected. She knew him a boy and a man, and a person able to speak with God. And in that moment, for the first time in Grace's life, she worshipped. O she would have done anything for him. She wanted to hold his hand and walk with him. She wanted him to come into her family and to heal all that was wounded there. His gentle demeanour, his calm words, his understanding and kindness and sensibility and the ease with which he found solution, Grace wanted it all to sooth like a balm.

More than this, much more, Grace wanted to follow him. She yearned to be by his side. To sit with him by the fire in the sand of the village; to hear his stories, to wander the lands. To look into his eyes; eyes that she was certain would know her even though, she admitted, she barely knew herself. Grace's whole heart ached to be seen and loved by that man. A man who was unlike all other men in her young life.

Grace was certain that if she could only find her way to him he would see her, and he would love her. Such was the power of this reading encounter. It rained sunshine upon that seed within her, an invitation to actively partake in its fruits, though it would be another thirty years before she fully embraced it. Praise God that his patience and guiding hand would continue to lead her as she journeyed back to her one true love.

# 10

# God Consciousness

As a child being read Bible stories by her mother, which were reinforced by Mrs Williams and the garage Bible Club, and then by going to church, God-consciousness was readily established in Grace. She had the capacity to conceptualise thought related to creation and a Creator. She was not only able to conceive of God, but was able to formulate thoughts about God, what God meant to her and what she believed in relation to God.

Grace developed this God-consciousness early in life. It began with the unseen realities of the non-material world; a world that through the reactions of others she realised was little spoken about or understood.

Like most children, Grace forgot about this natural world as she entered school and the pathways of brain activity and consciousness took on the cultural norms of her environment. However, a propensity towards the mystery of life remained with her. She wondered about the machinery and organisation behind what could be seen and experienced. She questioned, verbally and silently, seeking answers to a pressing force within her that asked ,'Why?'

For many, it is a quick path to awakening or a reaffirming of something they were born into through family religion. For others, like Grace, God is a walk of discovery, a slow journey of searching, often in the dark, for the hand that is reaching down to lift a person up. A hand that is never withdrawn.

Many, like Grace, explore various spiritual appetites. Often different pathways are entered into and sifted through. Some experiences assist to lift a person up in their pathway home to God. Others lack the depth, elevation, harmony and most importantly, the truth that is required when embarking on the journey towards union with God.

How a person meets God may differ between people. What happens when someone clasps ahold of that divine offering will vary depending on when in life the invitation is taken up. But ever and always, if earnestly sought, a person will come to know and to seek God.

For Grace, there was a long season between being God-conscious and God-seeking. She had dismissed God, so much so that by the age of sixteen and seventeen, she did not believe in God.

Grace knew there was symmetry in the world. She had experience of what she thought of as unexplained happenings and phenomena, with synchronicities she called coincidences that hinted at a creative pattern. But the pain of that early church rejection had developed in her a cynicism about Christianity. She started to question the history of the Church, the persecutions of peoples by the Church, particularly women, and the validity for the historical accuracy of Jesus. A rising sense of injustice arose in the teenager as the gap widened between her and the man she had so loved and wanted to be like in the book so carefully planned to come her way. Jesus, the Bible, all things Christian were far removed from Grace's sense of possibility now.

Yet God had sown good seed in her. Seed that took time to settle into the fertile soil of her pedigree. Seed that had to be patient for spiritual light and water, but which grew ever so slightly under the watch-care of an unseen ministry. For it was only by God's nurturing of that seed over the years that when the great reveal occurred in Grace's life, she was able and was ready, to receive its truth.

Now, in 1982, as a fourteen year old, Grace was not interested in God though God was interested in Grace. Very purposefully, three young girls were given to Grace as friends. By the grace of God, two kind and patient Christian girls, Jenny and Katie had befriended her at high school, while her dear friend, Stella was Greek Catholic with a rich display of Christianity in her home. One day after school, Grace, Jenny and Katie all sat on the school wall together talking about God.

'How can you believe in a man in the sky with a long white

beard ruling over everyone?'

Grace knew she was being extreme but her sense of hopelessness wanted to push hard to get answers.

Katie and Jenny looked at each other, unsure which one of them could respond.

Jenny, in her usual gentle manner said, 'Grace, we don't really think of God as a man in the sky with a long white beard. We think of God as a loving Creator who cares about us all.'

'Yeah,' Katie joined in, 'and we believe that God sent his son, Jesus, to die for our sins.'

'Sin. There's that word again.' A flash of the church minister of her childhood came to mind. 'But what is sin?'

'Sin means anything that we do wrong, like lying, stealing, or hurting other people,' Katie chimed up.

Grace went quiet.

Haven't I done all of those things? She thought.

Flashes of running from the local supermarket with chocolate bars tucked into her zip-up pullover made the girl grimace with guilt. I must be full of sins, she lamented within.

From that place of dejection, Grace launched another attack. It came from the growing sense of desperation she felt in trying to understand life and God, two seemingly incompatible things.

'Well, it's more than just the bad stuff we do, Grace.' Jenny saw the disheartened expression on her friend's face.

'Sin actually means that when we do those things, we're not in the love of God. We're so far away from Him.'

'Look, it doesn't matter.' Grace's ears had blocked up at the thought of being judged. 'That's not even the worst part. What's the whole "beam me up Scottie" thing that you all believe. I mean, Jesus just rose up into the sky and vanished. Like Captain Kirk from Star Trek in the transporter?'

Grace's friends looked at each other. They were patient, but they struggled for words to explain what they themselves had been taught, and had not questioned or really ever given much thought to. The resurrection and ascension were just as much a mystery to them as to Grace, only they believed both as part of their faith. They had no doubt that Jesus *was lifted up* and *taken up into heaven.* They didn't need to know the hows or the whys. They understood this as Jesus returning to God the Father, with a promise to remain in their lives, and to return.

'He went into heaven,' Katie said finally.

'Yeah, but how? And where?' Grace insisted. 'I just can't see how that is possible. I really want to know.'

Grace really did want to know. She yearned to feel some hope. To lean into that hope of something kind, wondrous and supernaturally promising of good in the world.

'Well, the Bible says that Jesus was taken up into heaven in a cloud, and that two angels appeared to the disciples, his main followers, and told them that Jesus would come back again in the same way.' Katie said matter of factly.

Jenny added context. 'I think it's really important to remember that the Bible isn't a science textbook. It's not trying to explain how Jesus's ascension happened in a scientific way. It's simply telling us that Jesus went to heaven to be with God.'

'Ah, ok. So, it's a mystery?'

'Yes, I think it is. But that's part of what makes it so amazing. It reminds us that God is beyond our understanding, and that He can do things that we can't even imagine.'

Grace stopped to think. He can do things we can't even imagine. That sparked hope in the girl.

'So what about the life after death thing?'

'You mean, eternal life?' Asked Jenny.

'Yeah, what's that about?'

'Well, when Jesus died on the cross to pay for our sins so that we could be forgiven, he gave us eternal life.' Jenny and Katie nodded in unison.

'But what is eternal life?'

'Eternal life is life that goes on forever, after we die. It's a life of peace and joy and love, with God.'

Though the girls' comprehension of eternal life was yet young, something splendid came over Jenny as she spoke these words. Grace noticed it. It was as if her friend became lighter. Brighter. As if the words themselves had luminosity that when spoken lit Jenny up from the inside. Her red hair and freckles, and green eyes hidden behind thick rimmed glasses, seemed to all brighten. A gentle smile came to her as she felt the warmth of the third person of the Trinity of God, the Holy Spirit, upon her.

'That sounds nice,' said Grace, and then a little shakily, 'but I don't know if I believe it.'

'I know,' said Jenny. She looked at Katie. 'We get that. It's a lot to take in. But it's all we've ever known, and we believe it because we've experienced God's love in our own lives.'

Still full of the grace of the divine light, Jenny's hands reached out to Grace. 'And we want to share that love with you.'

'I appreciate that. I really do. But I need some time to think about all this.'

'We understand.' The two nodded together again. 'We're here for you whenever you're ready.'

'Thanks.' Grace hopped off the wall. 'I'll see you later.'

She walked away, leaving Katie and Jenny sitting there. They watched her go, feeling a little sad for their friend. They knew that Grace was searching for something, and as much as they wanted to bring her into the warmth and love of God, they knew it was a journey that she insisted on taking herself. They couldn't convince her. They could just be themselves, and pray that Grace would find her way with God.

Grace left her friends feeling let down. Despite her argumentative stance with them, she wanted her friends to convince her. Beneath the skeptic facade, Grace hoped for explanations that would let her believe. She was desperate for the beauty of Jesus' life to be real and true and possible to get close to, because otherwise the world was confusing and lonely.

Loneliness was a constant part of Grace's life. She felt an outsider, and though she had a small group of friends, she didn't feel like them. Pathos was a close companion. As was perplexity. Grace didn't understand the world or the ways people were in the world, and she often misunderstood common language, and people's intentions.

Grace's trust had been shattered many times. Her early experiences of boys and men had caused a solid wall of mistrust. She wanted Jesus to be different, to be honourable and honest, a man of the highest calibre with exceptional principles, who treated women well. But if she couldn't believe the Jesus story, why would she believe the goodness of the man.

Grace was still an innocent at heart. She took people literally and was confused by sarcasm. She expected people to say what they meant and to mean what they said. Instead, Grace found that people lied, they blurred the truth, they hid things from each other and themselves. This made it difficult for Grace to get close to people. She was wary and as some commented, 'disarmingly honest'. Grace couldn't see how a person could be anything else in the world if humanity wanted to live in and experience a creation of truth and beauty. And this is most certainly what Grace wanted.

As it stood, Grace saw no evidence of God in her life, not in her family, and none she could see in the small version of her world. And in her isolation, in her hurt, she placed all her disappointment and frustration, all the injustice she perceived in life onto God. If God was so almighty, why would he let bad things happen in the world. Surely, he would step in and make things right.

*I AM.*

God's voice remained unheard. Grace had too much cloud of pain to know that she was not alone. She couldn't hear God and she wasn't aware of the angelic ministry about her. She was unaware that God knew every aspect of her being and had a plan for her.

Neither did Grace know that she could ask God her questions. She could confide in him as her special friend. And he would answer. If she had known this, she would have understood that God doesn't cause pain. He doesn't make the hardships of life. He allows our trials in life for many reasons, not the least is that humanity values and protects freedom: The freedom to choose, and to fall down and to get back up.

A person has free will. And God, who is love, does not arbitrarily intervene in that will. As Grace would come to appreciate, by living trials, an individual has the opportunity to grow, personally, and in relationship with God. Trials and joys provide the chance to show compassion, to love others, to learn about forgiveness, and if chosen, to understand and to call on the redeeming and restorative power of Jesus' crucifixion.

Grace didn't know this yet. That Jesus took all her wounds upon himself when he went to that cross. Grace still dwelt in the pain brought about by worldly life. Sometimes she didn't even know why she experienced such pathos. At times, she would find herself crying inexplicably. As if she cried for all humanity.

There was a grief that lived inside of Grace, a grief that she could not explain. It was the indelible feeling that humanity had lost something. She had no idea that what she felt was the true meaning of 'sin', the separation of a soul from God. The original sin of humanity falling away from their relationship with God. Unknown to Grace, she cried for all the lost, those souls separated from the grace of God and the gifts that the divine union gave to a person.

It would be decades before Grace was sufficiently well versed in the wounds of human life and the healing routes to joy. She was only just beginning to enter into years of patterned behaviour where relating to others, and self, happens through layers of childhood wounding and experience. This human condition plays out over and over again in individuals, communities, and nations so that the truth of life cannot be discerned with any reliability.

The lens through which a person navigates their world is clouded over, created in a sense by the particles of dust of life's layering that cause disorientation. Into this collage of early life encounters, a child becoming an adolescent who embarks upon adult relations enters a repetitive cycle of behaviour, false perception, reaction, recovery, behaviour, misguided perception, and this doesn't change until something new enters the midst.

A new thing must alter the pattern of behaviour in a person. It must change thought, belief, and action if the world's sway is to be overcome. Often this is in the form of an epiphany. Sometimes it is personal revelation; revelation given by the grace of God, or mystical experience that creates in a person a whole new paradigm of thought. It is this new thing that is often prayed for or actively sought out. Sometimes, in the instance of Grace, it is a gift born of circumstance that permits divine intervention.

Grace was a teenager who needed direction. She had the spiritual capacity to receive and to respond to mystical experience. The seed of God-consciousness had been sown. A new thing was required now to fertilise that seed and to grow it into God-seeking within Grace. And that is exactly what happened next for the girl. The new thing came out of a tragedy. It was an unexpected loss that touched many lives, and instigated God-seeking in our teenager.

Grace would soon be standing at a critical juncture in her life, poised to either challenge or perpetuate those patterns of woundedness as heavenly gifts invited her into new ways of thinking and being.

# 11

# Tragedy in Drama

A year later, Grace approached her favourite classroom, the drama room, where she was greeted by the sight of vibrant posters adorning the walls of the hallway, each showcasing past productions. Anticipation swelled within her to think she would be in this year's play. The buzz of creative energy from the room greeted her as she entered. There were no desks in the drama room, much to Grace's pleasure. It felt like they were in a real theatre studio away from school.

As she walked in, Grace glanced around to see where her friend Stacy was seated. All the children were arranged in a semicircle, facing the centre of the room, where Mrs Brown stood, radiating warmth and enthusiasm.

Mrs Brown, a petite woman with fiery red hair and a contagious smile, effortlessly commanded attention as she handed out new scripts for the play they were rehearsing. Grace admired her unwavering dedication and the way she encouraged each student's unique talents. She was also the only female teacher at school who dared to wear trousers instead of a skirt or dress. This spoke to Grace of a woman who was strong in herself and independent, which the teenager admired.

Her classmates varied in appearance and personalities: Jake, with his lanky frame and mischievous grin engaged in friendly banter with Maya, her piercing gaze, quiet confident as their contrasting energies sparked off each other; Graeme with his oversized glasses and studiousness; Petra with her red painted fingernails that always got her sent to the headmaster’s office, except by Mrs Brown who pretended not to notice; Lucas, who acted as the class clown with his infectious laughter and untamed curls. Other children who she knew less, but who chattered away, excited to be away from the confines of a regular classroom. Grace quietly observed them all, relishing the diverse mix of characters and bonds that formed within the group over a single production.

Then she caught sight of Stacey. Stacey, was Grace's longest friend. They’d known each other since the first primary school Grace went to when the Gleesons landed in Australia. She was a fascinating blend of contrasting qualities. With her impeccable skills in drama, she effortlessly captivated both her peers and her teachers. Stacey's talent on stage was matched only by her unique sense of style out of school. She effortlessly adorned herself in artistic attire, meticulously combining colours, textures, and accessories to create ensembles that were both visually striking and thought-provoking. Beneath her expressive exterior, Stacey carried a quiet confidence that bordered on pride, but she was too nice a person to ever be hurtful.

While Stacey was not the most vocal person in a room, her self-assured demeanour spoke volumes and made it clear that she knew her worth and was unafraid to assert herself when necessary. As she sat there in the circle, Grace observed something different about her friend. Despite having walked to school together, Grace saw something then that she hadn't noticed as they accompanied each other for the half hour walk in. A sort of deflation. It wasn't enough to cause secondary thoughts in Grace or even to arouse curiosity, more a passing thread unattended.

Sitting cross-legged on the carpet opposite Mrs Brown, Grace was one of eleven excited girls and boys in the high-school drama class. O how she enjoyed drama class. It had become her sanctuary, a space where she discovered a true passion. It was here that she unlocked her hidden talent for acting and in particular playing roles that let her express a range of emotions usually contained. Many of the plays the drama class read had characters that portrayed spectacular amounts of human condition. Grace especially shone in roles where her character was morally martyred. Her rendition of John Proctor in Arthur Millcr's, 'Thc Crucible' awarded her the highest grade of all the schools in the state, and an invitation to the national drama academy. She relished the anguish and courage of her character's final words as he is falsely accused and about to be hanged:

'I have given you my soul. I will not give you my name!'

This role evoked in Grace all the sense of injustice she felt existed in the world, and she delighted in being able to give it expression.

On this particular morning, Grace was watching Mrs Brown as she called out student names and assigned the paragraphs each had to recite that week. Stacy, a usually lively and outspoken student, had been uncharacteristically quiet when Grace sat down beside her. Even now, she sat with her head down. It was most unusual for her. Some of the other students noticed it too and began to exchange curious glances, their whispers fading into uneasy silence.

As Mrs Brown continued to hand out the lines to be learnt, she bypassed Stacey. This did not go unnoticed by the class but no one said anything. No one that is except the sandy haired boy, Daniel, sitting next to the teacher and opposite Grace and Stacey. His back suddenly straightened. Grace caught his eye at the moment his thoughts became words. Pointing at Stacey, he declared,

'What about her?'

Mrs Brown, who could have heard Daniel whisper, he sat that close to her, ignored the boy, pretending not to hear him. Instead, she continued speaking with enthusiasm about the casting of roles for the play. As she did, the atmosphere in the classroom shifted. Time seemed to slow down, and a hushed anticipation filled the air. The other students began to notice Stacey's uncharacteristic silence, their curious gazes darted between her and their drama teacher. Whispers rippled through the room, as they tried to make sense of the situation.

Seconds ticked by, each one amplifying the tension. Jake and Maya exchanged puzzled glances, their brows raised in question. Others leaned in, straining to catch the faintest hint of what might be happening. The room was consumed by a palpable sense of tension.

Mrs. Brown, usually known for her warm and encouraging demeanour, avoided eye contact with any of them. She looked from the papers in her hands up to the space in the room and back to the papers, shuffling them as she spoke. This did not go unnoticed by the students, who were accustomed to her focus and particular attention to detail.

Something was amiss, and neither Mrs Brown or Stacey were letting on. Stacey remained very still, her eyes not moving from the carpet. Her uncharacteristic silence spoke of something completely at odds with how she usually was, and how the students generally experienced their drama class. In this strangeness, the room became a microcosm of mixed emotions—curiosity, worry, and a tinge of fear. It was as if everyone was now holding their breath. Everyone that is except for Daniel.

Turning himself so that he bent forward and in front of thc teacher, he persisted. Having nudged a co-conspirator on the other side of him who nodded frantically, he now shouted in her face, 'MRS BROWN, how come Stacey doesn't get any homework? It's not fair.'

Mrs Brown frowned at the loud boy just as Stacey jumped to her feet. Grace looked up at her friend and then at the teacher. What is going on? She wondered. Turning to her friend, she saw a face she hardly recognised, distorted with something she couldn't place. Her eyes were full, watery with tears that didn't fall, and her face was red with emotion, but she was eerily calm, almost rigid.

That moment is captured now, frozen on Grace's memory screen. All the class was blurred except Mrs Brown, Daniel, and Stacey. They are all caught between movement, reaction and thought. Mrs Brown with mouth open, face reflecting rapid thinking and onset of shock. Daniel, half-way between indignant expression and a rising shade of pink. Stacey, standing very still, with something like challenge in her eyes now. All this was captured in one shutter movement over Grace's retina. Stacey had spoken. Grace, still looking at her friend, watched her for something: A smile to indicate she was joking. But nothing. She kept looking, waiting. Surely, any moment now Stacey would laugh. But she did not laugh and Grace continued staring at her friend as Stacey's words floated around the room.

'My father just killed himself didn't he.'

Angels nearby moved closer to their charges. They were prepared for this moment. Holding them steady, one or two came close enough to touch their child in a way that impressed heavenly light. For some it was comfort. For others that light stimulated the circuitry in their person so that a new thing emerged. A thought arousing a series of thoughts and spiritual illumination. A contemplation that lent itself to a growing change in trajectory. An idea that led the child to search for meaning, contributing to the birth of God-seeking. As happened in that moment for Grace.

Another shutter movement and the room was released. And then, pandemonium. Stacey abruptly turned around and ran out of the class room.

Mrs Brown glared down at Daniel. She called, 'Stacey wait!'

She got up and ran after the girl, issuing a 'Go to lunch' over her shoulder.

The children began to whisper. Gradually their volume increased equal to the back of Mrs Brown disappearing beyond the drama room door. Grace sat there stunned. Stacey's dad killed himself, she thought. Grace played over the morning they had shared together. They had walked to school. Yes, she had been quiet but sometimes Stacey was like that. It's partly what drew the girls to one another. Moody and deep they would acknowledge of themselves. Soul sisters, deep as the ocean. Grace smiled. But she didn't say anything.

Grace became lost in the reasons Stacy might not have confided in her, but she was interrupted by a crowd gathering around her. A multitude of questions battered her from other students. She could only make out one or two words here and there. Each insisted Grace should know the details of Stacey's declaration.

'Is it true?', '...kill himself?', '...lying', What happened?', 'Tell us', 'You're her best friend.'

Grace remained looking down, not really noticing who said

what. Slowly, numb to the barrage, internally replaying the scene over in her mind, she got up and without a word, picked up her school bag, turned and walked out of the classroom.

Her friend was off school for two weeks. When she got back Stacey told Grace that her dad had hung himself.

Grace had known Stacey nine years and had never met her father. He hadn't lived with them for many years.

When Grace asked Stacey why she had not told her about his death, Stacey simply replied, 'Well, it was no big deal. He was awful wasn't he? It wasn't important.'

And that was all there was to it. Grace let her friend be. That was also something they shared: Each girl knew when to talk and when to be silent.

Many years later, in their late twenties, Stacey shared more about her father with Grace. Billy was a war veteran. The horror changed him so that he drank alcohol to excess. And when he drank he would hit her mum. Stacey and her younger brothers were often present at these times.

Knowing Stacey's history helped Grace appreciate her initial response to her father's suicide. But at sixteen, Grace could not understand it and she wrote a poem about how devastated she would feel if her own father was suddenly gone from her. This poem expressed much of Grace's sense of alienation from her father. The poem was called, 'Why did you leave dad?' It would lead to the pivotal experience in Grace's life and her relationship with the indwelling Spirit of God.

# 12

# Meeting God

Grace wrote her poem, 'Why did you leave dad?', in class at school the day after Stacey's tragic announcement. When she arrived home her grandparents were visiting. Agnes and Donald had emigrated from New Zealand to Australia three years prior, and Grace delighted in having them so close. At seventeen years of age now, she had little memory of her early years living with them, but their care and love had become part of Grace's being. For the remainder of the Gleeson's time in New Zealand, Grace had stayed frequently with her grandparents on the weekends, and even now with them living in Australia, Grace stayed with them from time to time. Agnes and Donald were more like parents than grandparents and she thought it quite natural to be spending so much time with them.

Every now and then she would recall how sad she had been when they would visit Australia and have to return to New Zealand. Grace would stand in the airport, looking through the glass windows to the plane on the tarmac, tears streaming down her face. International telephoning was too expensive, so Donald would make cassettes of their news and send them to the grandchildren. Grace adored hearing their voices. She smiled every time she remembered again that they were not leaving but now lived in Adelaide. The family was all together.

On this Thursday, Grace came home, putting her school bag in her bedroom, and going into the kitchen for something to eat. Her father and grandfather were in the lounge room watching the television. Nancy was getting dinner ready while Agnes sat in the open plan dining room talking with her daughter. Grace asked if the two women would like to hear her poem, and they stopped what they were doing to listen. Sitting propped up on a stool between the dining area and the kitchen, Grace read aloud to them. She was quietly pleased with it, though there was a stir within her, like a memory just out of reach.

When she finished the poem that ended, 'Oh why did you leave dad?', she saw that her grandmother was crying. Grace was secretly pleased that her words had evoked such emotion from her usually quite stoic grandmother. Both women told Grace how lovely it was and Grace explained that it was about Stacey's father.

Later that evening when her mother was saying goodnight to Grace and Melody in the bedroom they shared, Grace said, 'I'm sorry I upset grandma with the poem, mum.'

'It wasn't that sweetheart,' said Nancy. 'Grandma got a letter today saying that Jimmy died last week.'

Grace couldn't help the teenage disappointment that it wasn't her poem after all that elicited her grandmother's tears, but she quickly put Brother Pride back in his place.

Not Jimmy, she thought. She knew how much her grandma loved her favourite brother, and Grace had grown to love him through her stories. It was Jimmy who bought his six year old sister a small elephant when he went to the local fairground and she hadn't gone along. This would prove to be the first of hundreds of figurine elephants Agnes would be given over the course of her long life.

Jimmy was her much loved and last remaining sibling. Once having emigrated from Scotland to New Zealand with Donald in their thirties, Agnes never saw her family again. Grace thought about her own loved ones and how painful it would be never to see her family again. With those thoughts, the scene was set for the evening's adventure, and for the new thing that God had planned for Grace.

Death seemed all around her. After her mother closed the door to her bedroom, Grace was filled with thoughts of loved ones dying. She remained wide awake even as Melody's breathing changed into sleep, an arm's length away in the next bed.

Grace let her thoughts run. She was curious. A series of questions floated through her mind. What is death? What happens to us? Do we live on? Or is it just the end?

Two things happened next. For the first time in Grace's young life, the proximity between her will and that of the Spirit of God within Grace moved within range of meeting. Grace remained unaware of this and those heavenly hosts attending her remained unseen. The second was the room became quite still. Grace was aware of her body lying beneath bed covers. She felt the soft flannel sheet around her exposed skin of hands and feet and neck. But there was a seeming distance between her senses and contact with her world. This distance in sensory consciousness helped her to let go of everything external to her. She no longer heard her sister's breathing, the clock on the bedside table between them ticking, the neighbour's dog barking or the remote voices of her parents down the other end of the house. The feel of bedclothes, pyjamas and even the cool night air on her face faded away. Grace blinked and shut her eyes, now enclosed in the not quite utter blackness that exists behind closed eyelids.

Something must live. A part of us must live, she thought.

Grace did not know where these thoughts came from, but they were a conviction she experienced as truth. And in that moment, the teenager made the decision that she would find the answers.

Grace decided to simulate death. To be clear, Grace was not suicidal and had no intention of ending her life. She did nothing to her body in the way of harm or injury. She let her thoughts journey to their end, and beyond. This seventeen year old schoolgirl wanted to study the point of death when the physical body ceases to live.

What would happen then? She thought.

Grace felt certain that some aspect of her would continue to live. She wanted to know the truth. She needed to know the truth. The pain she had witnessed in her grandmother's tears; the confusion and anger she had seen in her friend who lost her father, these had precipitated Grace's own concern.

What happens when they die? She kept thinking. And this naturally led her to ask, What happens to me?

Grace determined to find out.

There, lying in her bed, she let her thinking relax, refusing now to follow any thread of tangential thought. Her mind lightly floated as if in an ocean of restfulness. Methodically, Grace let in only those thoughts related to the point of death. She followed a stream of consciousness that settled on discovery, death, her death. She went to that last breath. She was in that breath. Her consciousness continued. Grace focused on separation from body. She imagined the essence of a person leaving the physical body, and focussed on that thought. By this very attention, her physiology responded. Her breath slowed, and became barely perceptible.

Grace turned her attention onto what she thought constituted the 'I' of herself. As she held that sense of 'I' in awareness, Grace proceeded to will herself, her 'I', to leave her body.

She had not been trained in consciousness studies. She knew nothing about out of body experiences or near death experiences. She was a teenager who had witnessed grief and wanted answers about death. It was her truth-seeking that propelled the impetus of this event.

So it was, to Grace's surprise that she began to feel an upward motion. It was as if her entire consciousness was moving, as happens with flight motion. This was followed by the sensation of rising above her bed. In the physical world, Grace did not move. She lay perfectly still, tucked in beneath her sheets, blanket and bedspread. Her eyes remained closed. She looked a picture of pure peace. If her sister had awoken and looked upon her, or her mother had entered the room to check on her daughters, Grace would have appeared to be pleasantly sleeping. But Grace was far from asleep. Indeed, Grace was in the midst of a very powerful spiritual awakening.

Within seconds of initiating the desire to leave her physical body, Grace became aware of looking down on her prone form in her single bed. From a distance of a few metres she could see her sister on the opposite side of the room and the bedside table between the girls' beds. Melody was peacefully asleep. Grace's heart expanded in love for her sister, even as she began to rise higher.

As the sensation of ascending continued, thoughts came to Grace, quickly and unbidden.

School. I won't have to go to school tomorrow. Ever again. She rose higher. Friends. I won't ever see them again.

Now, Grace moved beyond her house, and out into darkness that was at first a deep, expansive blackness, which held her suspended in upward motion.

Family. I'll never see them again.

For the briefest of moments, for a flicker, a pang of grief set to strike Grace. But before it could fully register, a warmth enveloped her, saturating her with joy. It felt familiar; an echo of the past, only not an echo, real and present. It was the same bubble of warmth from those early church experiences though this was magnified beyond anything she could imagine.

This warmth brought peace and something she could only put a word to the next day when she reflected on this moment: Completeness. No worry. No past. No pain. No striving or wondering. Only unity.

And then countless lights. What Grace had thought was a field of stars, all started moving towards her. So many. Twinkling like starlight, they approached her but kept a little distance. Grace could feel their curiosity. This host of celestial persons seemed to communicate with one another, and collectively and affectionately welcomed Grace.

And then came a greater love.

Love, Grace thought, and added, We need a thousand more words for love to describe this love.

Oh so mighty was this love that Grace felt certain she would buckle under its weight. The magnitude of it, the age of it. So full was she with its gift. And she knew it was a gift. A gift that permitted Grace to experience Itself. An embrace in which Grace at once felt very small, as if a little child, and yet as she naturally and wholly surrendered, she was upheld as uniquely, vitally, singularly special. As if she was the only person that existed. And yet, she felt part of the harmony of all those about her. She belonged. For the first time in her life, Grace felt… home.

Such was the magnificence of this divine proximity.

Grace was without thought in the majesty of the embrace, as if suspended, weightless in love. Then into that closeness, unseen, seemingly everywhere, within and without spaceless space, a deep, clear, voice resounded. It was unlike a human voice in tone and authority, and yet it was distinctly male.

In a most commanding, and gentle way, he said, 'It is not time Grace. Go back.'

And, as if his words themselves exacted the directive, Grace descended with a speed she could not track. No sooner had she heard his voice than she felt her consciousness whooshing backward, and there she was back in her body, in her bed.

Grace opened her eyes. A window between the girls' bed heads emitted a slither of light, enough to illumine to grey speckles the blackened room. Grace felt sure her sister would have heard the thud as she returned to body, but Melody was still asleep.

Grace lay very still. The connection of that divine embrace remained, but it was no longer all encompassing. She was no longer held in that warmth, and all sense of heavenly persons was gone. That was when she noticed it. The ache. It was deep and arresting. While it centred around the middle of her chest, she felt it in a place Grace had not known, and could not name. In one moment, she experienced the fall of humanity. Forbidden entry upon the path to Paradise, Grace's pain was cold, hard separation.

For an instant she had been utterly embraced, surrounded, encased in pure divine love. That embrace was more than someone's arms around her. In a human embrace, a person knows themselves distinct from the person holding them. Each body is uniquely shaped. The tension in the hold differs in arms and shoulders. The turn and position of the head is particular to the individual and the closeness of physical touch depends on the familiarity of the huggers. None of this factored into the divine embrace. Within it, Grace and God were unified. All earthly concept of herself was suspended in as much as loneliness, shame, grief, blame, fear, none of this existed. Only unifying qualities existed: Humility, surrender, trust, loving curiosity, interest beyond judgement, openness and awareness of a covering of authority. Not an authority that rules harshly, but one whose mantel envelops and within which through Its very own being elevates consciousness into seeing beyond the world, knowing beyond reason, feeling beyond wounding, touch in the manner of musical notes, of vibration, of harmony. By grace, humanity is transcended in that embrace.

Now no longer wrapped in the arms of the Beloved. No longer held in the glory of Heavenly light. Alone, Grace's chest hurt with separation. With grief. Silent tears streamed down her face. This was death. Death in life. What she had experienced was life. Life in death. Deathless life. How she wanted to return to that embrace.

This separation, which magnified beyond measure the separation of her early childhood attachment was a pain that would remain with Grace for decades. But without knowing it, the union that defied all pain, the divine encounter and embrace, would be the propelling force in her life's journey.

She had heard the voice of God. But what remained with this seventeen year old was the knowledge that God knew her by name. Even as the Bible says, though Grace knew this not:

*O Lord, you have searched me and known me. You know when I sit down and when I rise up; you discern my thoughts from far away. You search out my path and my lying down and are acquainted with all my ways.*

A single sentence spoken into her mind—'It is not time Grace, go back'—originated from beyond herself. The speaker of that sentence identified her name and knew her from the inside out. Here was someone who actually knew the depths of her. She was sure of it. Someone who could see her pain, her joy, her curiosity, her desperate desire to be loved. In this one embrace, Grace felt seen and known in the most complete way.

And in that one sentence, a future was alluded to when it would be time to experience that heavenly and celestial meeting in full. There was a timing for things she was not privy to knowing, and circumstances surrounding the architectures and structures that determined that timing that she could not possibly guess at. This excited our Grace.

That bubble of warmth knew the future—knew her future. It

filled her with hope and lit a fire in her for the readiness of that meeting to happen now. Grace came away from that encounter believing in a right time for everything. A destined time. She now understood that there existed a right and harmonious way for events to unfold, and that the factors of that unfolding were the domain and providence of unseen forces. And that humans could mess that timing up with their pushing, grasping, strength of will that went against the grace of that perfect timing.

By this experience, Grace's world was now divided, not only into interior and exterior, but into earthly-physical and spatial-celestial. Worldly and unseen. Human and divine.

One of the great challenges Grace encountered amidst all this reflection had nothing so much to do with timing, and everything to do with the 'Who' of the embrace. Who was it that enveloped her in such all-encompassing love? 'Who' was it that spoke? Who was it that knew her so completely?

Grace was still in a season of disbelief. As in she was not a believer. So much so that she avoided saying what she called the 'G word'. Despite everything, Grace was still reluctant to admit that it was God whom she met that night; that it was God who had spoken to her.

The tenderness, the affection and the authority of the voice told Grace that she was seen. She was known. Though she had felt alone in the world, she now knew that there was another with greater foresight, insight and awareness of life who, while resting in that grandness, knew her; not only knew her, loved her, and exuded such care and warmth for her as the most exquisite parent and friend. She knew it felt like the bubble of warmth of so long ago when she went to church, yet she still could not name it.

Grace had been touched by the divine embrace. And as she drifted to sleep that evening, every celestial associated with the blessed ministry of this revelation celebrated what Grace's encounter with God would mean for her life. They knew the magnitude of this unique event. The sublime embrace that Grace had been gifted would become the mobilising force in her life. It would be the stimulus behind all her subsequent decisions. It became the beacon, that although she had no destination co-ordinates for, she would hold as something to move towards.

This night, a night when Grace catapulted through the barrier of her regular thinking capacity into a new thing that was the realm of God, her spirituality was awakened. And to punctuate the promise of antiquity that is light breathing light through a flame more ancient than time, God planned another special meeting for his darling child.

# 13

# Dreams from God

In January 1986, Grace was nearly eighteen years old. It was summer with long days of hot sunlight. Only three months earlier, she had experienced the near death encounter, and heard the voice of God, clearly, palpably, near and lovingly. Grace had now begun to look beyond herself into the mystery of life. Prior to her meeting with the Spirit of God, her personal angst, comfort desires and needs, and the creative expression of those pangs had been self-centred. Grace now looked out into the world at its people and their lives, their pains and joys and workings. She now had a curiosity for knowing about the creation factors of her world and the people in it. She wanted to understand herself and others better, and mostly, she wanted to know more about the unseen fabric of the world.

Beyond the senses, beyond everyday concerns, beyond even the morality of life, Grace was now aware of a spiritual architecture.

While she couldn't yet speak about it in an authoritative way or identify its components or purpose, she felt the desire within, a drive seemingly familiar, to know and to experience more of that unseen reality. To this end, she began to ask meaning-of-life questions of her friends and of her mother. She started to write essays at school speculating upon the concept of fate and destiny. She was interested in history at school and the propensities of humans throughout the centuries to hurt one another and to war.

Grace had wanted to know why people were the way they were. Now she wanted to know 'what'. What drove people? What was behind behaviour and the patterns of history, her own and others. What was the mystery of creation that could not be seen but could be known and felt by the discerning individual as a pervasive presence in one's life? The divine embrace and its abounding love had awakened spiritual awareness. And she did not have to wait long before this spiritual awakening was reinforced.

So it was that Grace would have her second heavenly encounter, only this one would come in the form of a dream. Throughout history, God has and continues to speak into the mind of the sleeping person. Not to be confused with the everyday material of the workings of the mind or the fantastical nature of muddled dreaming, the divinely touched dream has a character all of its own.

In the Bible, God used dreams for divine communication to Abraham, Jacob, Joseph and many prophets giving guidance, leading, warnings and promises. The prophet Daniel had dreams and visions that revealed future kingdoms and events. Joseph received divine instruction warning him to take Mary and to flee to Egypt to protect Jesus from King Herod. When Jesus was on trial, Pilate's wife was given a dream of his innocence.

To know a dream is from God is to know yourself and the quality of your regular dreams, and to know what to expect of God and divine communication. God's dream has an entirely different flavour to the array of nonsensical dreams that a person is used to encountering. God's gift is spiritually directional. It speaks to an aspect of God's will for a person's journey towards God and possesses distinct qualities that set divinely given dreams apart.

A God-given dream is clear and vivid. It leaves an indelible mark on the dreamer's consciousness, touching a hungry soul rising up to meet it. These dreams not only convey God's intentions and plans for a person, but have transformative power merely by the divine energies that comprise the dream; energies that stem from God's essence. This proximity to God changes a person.

In many instances, dreams from God use symbolism to convey deeper meanings. Drawing inspiration from biblical figures like Joseph and Daniel, who interpreted dreams containing symbolic elements, these dreams may symbolise future events or spiritual truths.

As shown in Grace's dream, a significant aspect of dreams from God is their prophetic nature. Through dreams, God reveals future events or offers insights into the divine plan set for a person.

God's dreams also provide guidance and wisdom, functioning as a compass during times of confusion or uncertainty. They may offer a course of action, shedding light on important decisions to be made.

Dreams from God may also serve as confirmations or warnings, validating previous messages or affirming a particular course of action. They may also function as cautionary signs, highlighting potential dangers or negative consequences if certain paths are pursued.

In addition to their practical functions, dreams from God offer spiritual and moral encouragement. They bring comfort, assurance, and strength during challenging moments or spiritual struggles, serving as a source of solace.

When interpreting dreams from God, it is crucial to verify their alignment with biblical teachings and apply discernment. God's Word serves as the ultimate benchmark for understanding and deciphering these dreams, ensuring they are in harmony with God's character and principles as revealed in scripture.

Ultimately, dreams from God carry profound significance for the dreamer. By grace, they are a gift from God with a transformative nature that inspire spiritual growth, challenge limiting or outdated beliefs, and provide direction for fulfilling God's purposes. With their enduring impact, dreams from God leave an indelible imprint on the dreamer's life, evoking a sense of awe, conviction, and urgency. Our dear Grace gives testimony that God's dreams bear divine weight and importance, remaining etched in the dreamer's memory as a testament to God's communication and involvement in their journey.

And so it was, on a night in the summer of 1986 that God gave Grace a dream that would not only initiate the gift of prophecy and God-given visions in her life, but would become the life dream by which she navigated her world. It gave Grace a trajectory, insight into the journey towards a God-given goal and information about the unseen ministry that would accompany and lead her along the way.

The dream foretold tragedy and glory. In times of doubt this dream was her beacon, living in her soul, a reminder of what God had planned for her. These are the breadcrumbs, the leadings and seeds God plants in a person's life. They are especially recognisable amidst the lostness and worldly distractions in the life of a person who has no religious foundation, but who is hungry for meaning and spiritual revelation so as to understand the world and their place in it.

In the dream, Grace found herself standing in her high school sports hall, surrounded by a joyful celebration. The room was filled with adults and teenagers gathered around a man holding a baby. Grace felt a distinct sense of unease about the scene. The man held the baby out to her, and as Grace reached to touch the child, it disappeared. The room then erupted into chaos as the man, now wielding a machete set about menacing everyone with it.

Grace fled in terror, running towards her classroom for safety. She reached the door to her room, thinking she was safe, and as she went to turn the doorknob, a hand covered her own. Fear gripped the girl. Frozen, she kept her eyes straight ahead. With renewed courage coursing through her veins, she swung around to confront her pursuer, only to struggle to comprehend the sight before her.

Instead of threat or harm, standing there before Grace was Mary, Mother of Jesus. Bright and radiant, her loving smile touched a deep chord within Grace, thawing all her fear.

'You don't have to go in there,' Mary said, referring to the room behind the door.

Unbeknownst to Grace, it was not a place of safety as such, but a place of death. Within that room in her dream, the man had overpowered Grace, along with so many others. But unlike the spectres who appeared in the hallway in her sleep state asking Mary why Grace was not like them, Grace was not dead.

Blessed Saint Mary, Defender General, appeared before Grace in this God-given dream, as her intercessor. God loves humanity so much that he gave Mary to the world. And now she was here for Grace on behalf of God who calls the faithful to be a saintly voice and sight in the world.

In the dream now, Mary looked from Grace down the long hallway toward the end of the building. Grace followed her gaze. The end of the corridor was now obscured by the most luminescent of white lights. This light, like nothing Grace had ever seen, not sunlight nor electric light, lit up the entire length of the passageway, streaming out to her.

With great care, the Lord's Mother turned to Grace and very tenderly took ahold of her hand. With a purposeful smile, Mary faced Grace towards the light. Grace felt a deep peace come over her at the same time as Mary led her forward saying, 'It will be a long journey, and painful, but it will be worth it.'

Grace awoke from this dream and lay in her bed completely still. As still as she had on the night she had visited heaven. Her breath hardly made movement in her body as she went over the dream again and again, committing it to memory. She leant down and retrieved the diary she kept by her bed and recorded each detail.

Grace vividly recalled Mary's appearance. Light seemed to shine from within her as well as about her from the brilliance of the light emanating from the end of the hallway. She seemed ageless, not in her late years and not young, but youthful in vitality. Her whole being emitted kindness and a motherly love and strength.

Grace knew in the deepest part of her that what Mary spoke was the truth.

The Spirit of Truth registered this upon her soul, whispering, *I have much more to say to you, more than you can now bear.*

Grace was already being lead towards that light.

This was the aspect of the dream that upon waking, Grace focused on, not the terror or the man with the knife and the vanishing baby. Even a decade later when the tragedy of this event played out for real in her life, Grace didn't make the link between the prophetic insight of this dream and what had become her reality. It was not until late in life, a childless woman now familiar with the Light of Christ and God's promises, that Grace made the connection. And when she did, she wept. O she'd wept before for the loss of her baby, but now, clear eyed, aware that God had forewarned her of events to come, she read the scriptural passage of Jeremiah with new eyes—*Before I formed you in the womb, I knew you.* And brokenhearted, truly repentant, she wept again. A whole of body weeping and gnashing. Only God could ease that pain. Not any words of consolation from people. Only God's love, forgiveness, and compassion provided reassurance for Grace in her times of grief and reach for healing.

*The Lord is merciful and gracious, slow to anger and abounding in steadfast love...He does not deal with us according to our sins nor repay us according to our iniquities...as far as the east is from the west, so far he removes our transgressions from us.*

Here and now, Grace had no head or heart for the full significance of God's gift of Mary to her that night, or what the promise of the Light of the World would mean for her. God knew that Grace had a whole lot of waywardness that she would experience first, lostness and sin, separating her from God, before she would understand the divine message of this dream:

*For once you were darkness, but now in the Lord you are light. Walk as children of light, for the fruit of the light is found in all that is good and right and true.*

Grace only heard Mary's words and the promise of something better in life. What, that light was, Grace didn't know. What Grace held to now as fact was the promise. A heavenly promise that whatever she underwent in life, no matter how painful, it would all be worth it in the end. She had no guarantee of it, no evidence for it, no reason to think that it was true, except that now, without doubt, she believed.

This was the first and only time Saint Mary featured in one of Grace's dreams, and she dreamed prolifically each night. It was a dream like none other and she could never even recall thinking about the mother of Jesus. So she had no reason to think Mary would appear in one of her dreams. Yes, this dream felt different to other dreams. It was clear and vivid. It met the qualities inherent in a dream given by God, not that Grace knew what they were, only that she knew it wasn't one of her regular dreams. It was real. And Grace, focusing on Mary's words, knew them to be true. Unequivocally, Grace believed that something wonderful awaited her, and that she was taken in hand now and would be led towards that light. Yes, Grace believed this with her whole being.

# 14

# Young Affections

To have faith, one must believe but a person might believe and yet not have faith. To know faith, to live by faith, and to understand faith as a gift of grace from God is a foundation for spiritual living in the world. When a person lives by grace and faith alone, there becomes a symbiotic relationship between that person and God. To live in accordance with the mandates of heaven, by the laws of heaven and by the grace bestowed upon the individual life by the very fact of that life, by the ultimate source of life, the Creator, is in essence to live with God. That is faith, true faith.

It is not something a person strives for or works for or is given as reward or withheld as punishment. Rather, faith lived in union with God's will is quite simply the turning towards God. It is seeking out God, finding God, and then permitting oneself to be what God made a person to be, and that is, like God. Grace had not yet come to live such faith or union.

Grace believed in something. She considered that something to be sympathetic to her, to humanity, but she had no way of entering into relationship with that something. For her, the force, the power, the existence of that something was 'out there', unapproachable in person or as a person, merely a stream of unimaginable currents producing order, symmetry and unfathomable in nature, yet able to effect changes on the smallest, largest and personal scale. She believed that something was good, and specifically that it wanted good for her, and would guide her in that goodness.

Unfortunately, the 'something' that Grace believed in could not be approached for help or healing or prophetic insight. There was no Holy Spirit in Grace's schema of life, only signs, patterns and a benevolence. Well, none of this aided Grace when she entered into relationships, caught in the snare of affect brought on by woundedness.

Our darling was yet to have a boyfriend, unlike many of her friends. Throughout high-school she liked one boy, Angelo. Her friends knew she liked him, and Angelo's friends knew he liked her. On the one occasion that they shared a note of affection between themselves, someone found it and made fun with it. They wrote no more notes.

Angelo was Greek, and Grace, while she was accepted by the Greek community at school and befriended by many, still, she was not Greek. Both she and Angelo knew that this cultural divide meant they could never be together. He must marry a Greek girl. So, Grace didn't date any boy. And Angelo didn't date any girl.

This obstacle to romantic happiness didn't stop Grace imagining what it would be like to kiss Angelo. At night when her sister was asleep in the bed opposite her, she would press her thumb and forefinger together in the shape of lips and practice kissing… just in case.

Well, just in case came about on the night of the prom in their final week of school. Grace was with her friends, some of them in the Greek group that kept together. Angelo was sitting against the wall with a row of boys. It was dark. The music was playing. Grace's friends encouraged her to ask Angelo to dance. She was too shy, so in the crowds they corralled their friend towards the boy, and at that unsuspecting moment, pushed Grace into Angelo. She fell right into his lap. While Angelo's friends and Grace's friends let out raucous laughter, the boy in focus didn't say a word, but dextrously repositioned Grace so that she sat on his knee.

They faced each other now. Eyes locked. Five years of attraction from age twelve to now going on eighteen lit a fire in them. His fingers laced within hers. Something tingly happened in her body. Their faces were close now. She could smell a hint of garlic on his breath. Mustering up all her courage, Grace lent forward to kiss him. Angelo leaned in to meet her lips.

Sometimes, practice does not make perfect. Grace opened her mouth as she'd seen in the movies at the same time as he opened his, obviously having watched similar films. There and then their teeth collided and their foreheads banged together. Her bottom lip bounced off his top lip, encasing his nose so that he squealed a little and lent back.

Grace jumped up, ran off and hid herself in the crowd. Humiliated and terribly disappointed, she kept her distance from him for the rest of the night.

At school the next day they passed each other going from one class to the next. Grace forced herself to look up as he walked by. He slowed and gave her the sweetest smile. Her eyes lit up and spoke into his heart, both of them acknowledging a chance of something missed.

The siren rang for class to commence. Angelo hurried on while Grace watched him go until he turned a corner. That was the last she saw of Angelo. He graduated and left school. Grace went full-time in the supermarket as Office Assistant, and Angelo became a part of school history.

Some years later Grace learnt that Angelo had married Grace's close friend Sophia Alexopoulos. Sophia was the most beautiful girl at school, not because she was pretty, though she was, with her long black hair, and not because she was smart, though she was, but more because Sophia had the beauty of a kind heart. She was polite and quiet, sweet and caring, looking after her brother who had autism. Yes, Grace had smiled to know Angelo found a nice Greek girl, and she was genuinely saddened later in life to learn they had divorced. Occasionally, she would wonder about what might have been, and smiling, would whisper, 'Thanks be to God.'

Grace couldn't know then that when a person becomes a spiritual seeker, they're actually looking for that light that is within them. The light that reflects God in them.

When that seeking begins, and the desire for a divine friendship emerges, it can be difficult in the world. There is a yearning to be in perfect union with the life of the interior without knowing that is what the great desire is. Humanity looks to other people to fill that longing, that search. Great marriages and partnerships are formed this way, but great suffering is met too by those whose feelings and behaviours are marred by fragmented childhood relationships. Like a thief in the night, for those people the world can come in and steal jewels bestowed upon a person by God. Though Grace had no words for this truth yet, she knew it in her heart, so that though she entered relationships, she sought to keep herself for God.

At the tender age of nineteen, our Grace stood at the crossroads of matrimony, contemplating a life with a young French sailor, Jacques. Little did she know that her mother had stood at a similar juncture at the same age, though their outcomes were quite different.

Walking down the Adelaide mall one evening, two sailors met two young Australian girls. Jacques and Grace were drawn to each other immediately. Dark hair cut close to his head, with wisps of curl on his forehead, accentuated thick black eyebrows and oceanic eyes that reflected the stormy passion of Mediterranean seas. With olive skin toned against deep blue and white striped uniform, of similar height and a polite, chivalric manner, Grace was at once smitten.

Jacques was sweet. Shy, with few words. Grace had high-school French, he little English. What they met in each other was a purity of heart, a poetic innocence and a pain for love. All this in a week of knowing one another.

Winds of romance swept through their souls, igniting a flame that burned brighter with each passing day. They walked together, danced, played bowls, laughed and held hands.

On the eve of his departure, friends drove them back to the port to where his battlecruiser was docked. Sitting quiet in the backseat of the car, his hand reached for hers, their fingers intwined with tender caresses. They were as two celestial bodies gravitating towards one another. While their companions chatted on, Jacques and Grace were lost in the sensation of touch, and in a melancholy of reverie for the week they had shared; a joy that was about to end.

In the hushed sanctuary of their place in the vehicle, Neil Diamond's mellifluous voice gave song to their heart's plea in the melody of 'Hello Again'. With each beat of their hearts, a rhythm united in tune now, with the essence of the song's lyrical truth, their hands gripped tighter in longing.

Standing at the on-ramp to the battle cruiser, Le Colbert, they clung to each other. Tears, glistening like dewdrops on fresh grass traced delicate paths down their cheeks. It was a tender moment. The world was lost to their embrace. Until a shrill whistle blew. A naval officer close by, whose look said, 'I understand', spoke a word in French to Jacques, who nodded but clung tighter to Grace. And then let go. And then he walked up the ramp, waved, blew kisses, and was gone.

And Grace cried all the way home.

Jacques wrote every week from every port. He sent gifts and love letters, and Grace felt so blessed. In one letter, two years later, Jacques proposed to her, offering a home for her with him in France together. Grace was torn. Her heart swooned to think of Jacques, and readily leaned into a rural life in France with him. But there was something inside her that whispered another destiny. She felt too young. There was still too much to do, to live, to explore, to know about herself and the world, to learn what it was that called her. So she broke his heart. And she didn't hear from him for a long time afterward, until one day she did, decades later. He was still sweet and charming, and thereafter, no matter where Grace was in the world, on the 6th of February, Jacques sent birthday wishes. She loved him for that.

After the innocence of Jacques, Grace fell into a series of disappointing relationships. She learnt that mature men wanted more than to hold hands, and despite her reluctance, Grace went along with their expectations. In secret, she felt impure and violated. Naively drawn to pleasing and rescuing people when she detected brokenness amidst goodness in them, she formed bonds with unavailable partners, and this held its own set of challenges and pain.

So many intimate encounters and relationships are formed on the basis of the brokenness in each person. Grace would be in her fifties before she truly understood the call of celibacy upon her, and had the strength and faith conviction to continue to live free from the passions of the flesh in the world—passions that separated her from God.

With no community of Christian sustenance to feed her burgeoning spiritual awakening, Grace fell asleep in the spirit. She lost sight of God, and Mary's hand was no longer palpable to her touch. The world came in and stole them from her along with Grace's innocence and wonder. Increasingly, our dear one learnt to hide a deep loneliness that was rarely expressed and even less often shared with anyone. She was desperate for companionship, for something to fill that hole; a hole the world had chiseled into her, a pit of separation and longing.

# 15

# Separation and Longing

How many people truly understand the depths of human longing and the ways in which a person tries to fill the void within themselves? How many people can relate to this struggle? These questions plagued Grace as she navigated life, searching for meaning and connection.

Grace, like many, sought solace in various distractions and temporary fixes to alleviate the pain of her loneliness. Television, novels, chocolates, intimacy, alcohol, drugs, fitness, diets, career success—she tried them all. Yet, no matter how many emotional fillers she indulged in, the emptiness persisted.

The cruel irony of human nature is that those who feel the most isolated and who long for connection are often the ones who struggle the most to forge genuine relationships. The wounds they carry and the societal structures that perpetuate their pain trap them in a cycle of isolation. This is the great downfall of humanity: A terrifying disconnection from all that God offers individuals and the species.

Grace came to realise this truth earlier than some, but later than others. In her younger years, she found solace in creative outlets like painting and writing, which allowed her to express her emotions and glimpse the deeper beauty she longed for in life. However, as she transitioned into adulthood, less constructive behaviours crept in, leading her down a destructive path fuelled by the deceiver, alcohol.

The use of alcohol became more prevalent from the age of nineteen. First, Grace drank to keep away feelings of lostness among friends and family. Then she kept a flask of alcohol near her, drinking in the evening and in the morning before work.

She began dating, and fell into a common misconception that intimacy equated to love and joy, and fulfilment. And found that it did not. Her need to be loved by her father led her to seek out older men as companions. Those men only saw the surface-level beauty she possessed. There was no sanctuary or reconciliation of heart found in those places for Grace, with those persons. Only heart break and degradation.

As Grace sank deeper into numbness, alcohol became her refuge, shielding her from thoughts and feelings. She stumbled into the nightlife scene, where she was vulnerable and oblivious to the dangers that lurked in those environments.

In later years, Grace found herself counselling men and women who had experienced brutalisation or had lost family members to violence. Some of her clients had fallen into the depths of alcoholism or drug addiction. During these moments, Grace would reflect on her early adult encounters and remember her grandfather's poignant words concerning the deaths of his friends in the prisoner of war camp.'There by the grace of God go I'.

God inside Grace cried out a thousand, thousand times, *Grace. Grace. Turn around. I am here. Grace. Beloved of God. Child of Light. Turn around.*

But through the alcohol, Grace was too numb, too caught in the traction of familial and social pattern to hear or heed the One who could truly befriend her.

These years set the scene for Grace's need for repentance and forgiveness. She didn't know it then.

When the presence of God within draws close in a person, a sense of discord may be felt by the individual when their behaviour, thoughts and ideas are not in harmony with that truth that is the divine presence. Truth rises up within a person who has a gut feeling, intuition, a sense or knowing. It is an opportunity to choose differently, to take another approach, to step away, to cease a behaviour, to leave a relationship, to change a job that is not befitting of a destiny, to pay attention to the guiding light within a person that knows them in their most purest and true form, and who tries with all Its might to help each one know themselves too.

The pain of that discord is real. It is often stressful, confusing and disorienting. Of course, this is not the intention of the all-loving divinity within a person. Rather, the Spirit of God would have only what is best for someone. It is by the mere purity of that divine presence that human shabbiness is spotlighted and felt, not by all, but by those who have a healthy set of values and morality or whose conscience is able to self-correct or even question the current climate in them, while the same virtues and values are muted.

It was during these numbing years that her deceitful heart developed a severe resistance to God. Her days were filled with regular work. Her nights were carnage. She knew she needed help but she didn't know how to break the patterns of impetuses that gripped her with such cruel delight. And the fear of what existed without the filler, the distraction, the numbing device, kept her locked in an open-doored cage.

Such is the corruption of sin.

The concept of sin, understood as separation from God, played a significant role in Grace's life. She had unintentionally strayed and sin had snatched her from the invitation of God to bring her home. It wasn't deliberate. It wasn't wilful. Grace didn't seek to live such a life, but the world took advantage of her vulnerability and exploited the shadow that those hurts cast upon the footsteps she had taken towards the light.

In later years, Grace would discover in her therapy practice the degree to which people feel this separation and longing. Each experience is unique to a person's life situation, and yet, Grace saw similar themes. Like her, there was often a sense of feeling lost, not quite fitting in. Her clients felt hollow or empty. They described a hole or pain in their heart region, a pit inside and a deep sense of loneliness or isolation. Others felt alien, as if they didn't belong in the world. They asked what's the point? What's the meaning of it all?

At the age of twenty-four Grace reached a tipping point and sought some help. She went to the family doctor and asked for a referral to help her understand her relationship patterns. In her pursuit of self-understanding, Grace saw a psychiatrist and other counsellors. Through therapy and introspection, she began to unravel the psychology behind her behaviours and the impact of her past experiences.

While the patterns didn't completely disappear, her newfound awareness allowed for moments of clarity. There were times when Grace could identify when she was caught in the snare of acting out a need derived from early parental attachment separations or from fear based on those teenage assaults. This knowledge and awareness gave her greater choice.

In these early years of self-discovery and finding her way, Grace's choices were still limited by the repercussions of life and she remained deaf to the divine voice within, but she began a life of redemption, writing letters to any person she may have hurt along the way.

The healing that Grace entered into began to free her from layers of misguided attachment that steered her away from the plan God had for her.

God understands that the soul of a person longs for growth and union with the divine, and that *a longing fulfilled is sweet to the soul.* That is why God sent Jesus Christ as a human incarnation of divinity—to show people how to come home to God. Jesus serves as a roadmap, an example, and a guide to a person's divine ascension. In Jesus, humanity has been given the greatest gift to free themselves from the past, heal, and embrace a future aligned with eternal life.

God is ever calling each person home to a union of wills, presenting individuals with opportunities to respond to this call. These moments of grace invite a person to choose whether to deepen their connection with God or rely on their own ways and understanding.

Often, individuals make decisions based on their comfort, security, pleasure, or to alleviate fear, which is what Grace had been doing for some years. Sometimes, these choices are masked in righteousness, as individuals unknowingly engage in habitual rituals, superstitious beliefs, or anxious thoughts and behaviours. These tendencies, rooted in accumulated experiences and survival instincts, perpetuate the state of separation from God.

Grace's story highlights that separation clearly. Only now, as she floundered, she also reached for help. Grace actively wanted a change in her life. She knew that there was more for her than what she had settled for, and stumbled into time and again.

While all the relational therapy was happening, Grace had a cervical cancer scare that ended in a minor surgery. She told few people other than her parents and her manager at her work who needed to know why she required the time off she'd requested. It turned out that he was a Mormon. He sat down with Grace and spoke to her about God, and shared his belief that all would be well for the young woman.

'God has plans for you,' he said

Grace appreciated his word, and without taking the invitation to explore Mormonism further, she remained uplifted.

This health scare also brought with it a personal perspective of the finite nature of human life. Grace was resolved not to waste her one life. A year and a half after her surgery, in a new job that didn't help her use of alcohol, Grace was ready for change. And though she didn't know how to extricate herself from the world she had entered, she didn't have long to wait before a way was made.

Within a matter of weeks, she was let go from her job after lodging a sexual harassment complaint against one of the staff members. Rather than fight the injustice, Grace started anew.

She went home to New Zealand to visit her dad's mother, her nana, whom she hadn't seen for nineteen years. Grace was ever grateful for that opportunity. Martha died three months later. At the same time, Grace broke off an unhealthy relationship with a gambling man. And most importantly, two things: The first was a spontaneous healing gift given by God, the second was that Grace said, 'Yes', and agreed to uproot from Adelaide to live on a small island. It was there that her true spiritual awakening took flight.

# 16

# Chi Awakening

As the golden globe hung in a pristine sky over the Indian Ocean, Grace sighed contentedly. She stood on the edge of Fremantle, a port city nestled within the embrace of Perth's azure coastline. The air hummed with a blend of nostalgia and vitality, echoing whispers of times past. Quite like her hometown of Adelaide, sandstone buildings in the city stood tall, their weathered facades adorned with tales of seafaring adventures and convicts seeking redemption. Cobbled streets, lined with eclectic cafes and bustling markets, carried rhythmic footsteps of locals and visitors alike. Their laughter and conversations blended harmoniously with the melodic tunes of street musicians. The city was teeming with life, and Grace felt alive with it.

Now twenty-six years old, our Grace was a young woman. She had travelled to various states in Australia, returned to New Zealand to visit her nana before she passed, and made the great decision to leave her home again. And here she was, on her way, now in Perth on a layover before her morning flight to new horizons.

But before she left Australian shores, she had one small task to complete. She needed to find someone. Specifically, she sought a renowned Chinese medical practitioner. So, here she was making her way through coloured markets, food stalls, fruits and vegetables, hanging fish, barrels of spice, clothing racks, scarfs, trinkets, rugs and jewellery, Indigenous art, craft, tarot card readers and massage chairs,  musicians and ice-cream venders; all unlikely neighbours to one another. It was a splendid sight that made Grace nostalgic for the Adelaide Markets, and at the same time detached from it all, focussed on getting to the address she sought.

Weaving through the aisles at a steady pace, Grace threaded her way towards a side-street at the far end of the sprawling hall. Turning to the left, a block away and Grace looked down at the worn piece of paper she had carried with her these past days. She was there.

The door was open. She knocked and a male voice, said, 'Come in.'

Grace entered what appeared to be an office, a compact space adorned with a desk, a bookshelf, and a single chair. The place was small, providing just enough room for essentials. Grace could see through the open door opposite the desk a portion of a very large shop. Rows and rows of glass cabinets adorned the walls to the ceiling, with all manner of jars filled with unidentifiable objects. The overwhelming smell was pungent, spicy but not unpleasant.

As she walked in, Grace felt a flutter of excitement.

Answers, she thought. I've come for answers. And she was hopeful of receiving them.

Turning to the figure in the room, Grace looked upon a distinguished, middle-aged Chinese man seated behind the desk. Michael Wei looked up from his book, pages filled with intricate diagrams showcasing different upper body poses and lines of Chinese characters. A warm smile illuminated his face, accentuated by a well-groomed moustache and a neatly trimmed lower lip beard. He radiated warmth.

'Hullo, how can I help you?'

Realising that she was in a private office rather than the Chinese Medical Centre and shop, Grace hesitated.

'Oh sorry, I thought this was the Chinese Medical shop. I was hoping to speak to Mr Wei.'

'Yes, that is me. How can I help?' He repeated.

'I'm Grace.' The young woman smiled. 'I wanted to ask you about an experience I had recently,' then hastily added, 'with the chi, I think.'

Grace was on unfamiliar ground. She had only read about Traditional Chinese Medicine in the Adelaide library a week ago. One book she found seemed to shed some light on a strange phenomenon that had left her changed. Now that she was about to work in Indonesia, she was thrilled to find an expert in Chinese medicine in Perth where her plane stopped over before the morning flight to the island that would become her home for the next four years.

'Yes. Chi. Please tell me, what is it?' He said.

'Thank you. Well, a few months ago, I was standing in the hallway of my parents' house when I felt a surge of electricity rise up from my lower body and shoot through the top of my head. It was so powerful. It left me with a bit of a ringing head, but the strangest thing was that afterwards, I could still feel it. As if it remained within me, coursing through my body.'

As she spoke, Grace could feel the energy of her words reverberating through her body, reminiscent of the tingling sensations she had experienced during that transformative moment.

'I felt it coursing through my arms and legs, and down my spine, like a river of vibrant energy,' she continued, her voice growing more animated. 'It was as if my body was alive and dancing in warmth with tingling that seemed to rise up out beyond my skin.'

Now, Michael Wei had extensive knowledge and expertise in Qigong, Tai Chi, Taoism, and Chinese Medicine, and was a beacon in the Chinese Medical field in Australia and in China. Beyond the walls of his Perth based school, Michael Wei's influence extended far and wide. His reputation as a leader in Traditional Chinese Medicine earned him a place of respect within the most prestigious hospitals in China. Physicians sought his guidance, recognising the depth of his understanding and his ability to bridge ancient wisdom with modern medical practices.

Hailing from a lineage of revered masters, Master Wei's command of Qigong was unparalleled. He possessed an innate ability to harness and cultivate the vital life force, leading others to unlock their own energetic potential. His qigong school in Perth served as a sanctuary where students from all walks of life gathered to learn from his wealth of wisdom.

Under his watchful eye, a group of devoted medical students had the privilege of being mentored by him. With his patient guidance and profound teachings, he instilled in them a deep reverence for the principles of Traditional Chinese Medicine, inspiring them to become compassionate healers who honoured the holistic nature of the human body and spirit.

Amidst the accolades and accomplishments, Master Wei remained humble, always embodying the core principles of his teachings. Kindness radiated from his being. His demeanour was one of serene wisdom, and his gentle presence nurtured an environment of trust and growth.

Here, in his office, Master Wei's eyes widened, recognising the significance of Grace's encounter. He encouraged her to delve deeper into the experience, asking about the impact on her body and its internal organs.

'Please, continue,' he said.

'This energy seemed to stir the very core of my being,' Grace exclaimed. 'My body came alive, harmonising with the ebb and flow of… I don't know what it was, but it seemed like I was now plugged in, in a way I wasn't before. I know that sounds strange.'

Grace screwed up her face to indicate how preposterous it sounded to her ears, not the least because those family and friends around her had told her how weird it was.

Michael Wei nodded, but insisted, 'No, no, not strange. Very normal. But not normal for Westerner. What else?'

Grace was intrigued now. What did he mean, 'Westerner'? But she continued to describe the event.

'After this, I noticed that there was warmth in my body now. A kind of warmth that moved when I put my attention to it. And then, when I touched people that warmth seemed to go to them. They could feel it. Sometimes, they said it was soothing, and even quite healing.'

Then more to herself, she mumbled, 'Others said I was a freak.'

'Yes. Yes.' Michael Wei appeared quite excited.

Grace's heart sank. Oh, so I am a freak, she thought deflated.

'People make fun of what they do not understand.' He looked directly into her eyes.

Lifted up, Grace agreed, 'Yes. Can you tell me what this is?'

Grace was desperate to know she wasn't going crazy.

Master Wei nodded, his expression reflecting the wisdom of a teacher who recognised the magnitude of such experiences. For a moment there was silence as Grace and the Master shared a point of connection—an acknowledgement of the beauty and transformative power that now ignited the young woman's path of self and spiritual discovery. She was aglow in the fire of that energy now. And he could see that clearly.

‘Yes, Grace,’ he said, his voice firm in its authority on the matter. ‘What you have experienced is a spontaneous awakening of your chi, your vital life force energy.’

Grace took in a deep breath.

‘Chi? I've read about it in a book, but it seemed so mysterious. I didn’t really understand what it was. Is it real?’

Master Wei leaned forward, his eyes gleaming with enthusiasm and wisdom.

‘You have felt it Grace. It is very real.’ He stood up from behind the desk and walked over to a tall bookcase. As he spoke, he lifted out a heavy looking blue book.

‘Grace, Traditional Chinese Medicine includes chi and has a deep understanding of the human body and its systems.’

As Master Wei spoke, Grace noticed his heavy accent. In an English as second language way, the Chinese Master talked in clipped sentences, using easily understood words. Grace was grateful for this as she concentrated on his explanation of her experience.

‘Chi is mystical or unfamiliar to Westerners because Chinese approach has holistic view. Physical body, mind, and energy all connected.’

He paused, allowing his words to sink in before continuing, ‘When we say “chi”, we mean life force energy that flows through body. This energy is real force, can be measured and influenced.

Science now see how chi affects physiological and biochemical in body.'

Grace listened intently, her curiosity fuelled by Michael Wei's words. The merging of the mystical and the scientific resonated within her, as if two puzzle pieces were fitting together.

'For example,' Master Wei continued, 'study show acupuncture stimulate release of endorphins and neurotransmitters with physiological response to promote healing and no pain. Also overall well-being increase with chi movement.'

Grace felt a sense of relief and validation wash over her. The scientific foundation underlying the mystical world of chi provided a bridge between her Western upbringing and this spiritual experience.

'Thank you, Master Wei,' she said, her voice brimming with gratitude, 'but what causes it, and what do I do with it now?'

Master Wei's eyes sparkled with satisfaction, appreciating Grace's receptiveness to his explanation.

He nodded and replied, 'I never heard of spontaneous awakening in non-Chinese before. Very rare I think. Definitely, it is a good thing. You come to my classes. I help you develop this gift.'

Grace was at once excited and disappointed. Tomorrow she would be leaving with no knowing when she would return to Perth. Master Wei saw her mood change.

'I'm sorry Mr Wei, I am leaving Perth tomorrow. I have a job on Burnett Island—you've probably never heard of it, it's…'

'Yes, yes, good. Burnett Island', the Chinese Master walked back around to his desk and sat down with the book. 'I go every month. I teach qigong. You come to my class.'

Grace could not believe what she heard.

*And my God will meet all your needs according to the riches of his glory in Christ Jesus.*

'You go to Burnett Island?'

'Yes. Yes. Big Chinese community there. I go there and teach you.'

Grace was beside herself, overjoyed.

As she looked at Master Wei, she knew that this path, this new thing in her life, held limitless possibilities for growth and transformation. And with his guidance, she felt confident in her ability to navigate this world of chi, embracing its profound spiritual essence.

He stood up and handed Grace the blue book. Grace was delighted. In the introduction it mentioned her new Master as having revised the book and had a whole section on chi and qigong.

'Chi is the basic substance to compose the world and all matters in the universe appear by the movements and mutations of chi.'

In the context of medicine this viewpoint believes that chi is the fundamental constituent to form thc human body, and the movements and mutations of chi can explain all the physiological activities.

Grace felt so grateful. She was certain she'd been guided to Michael Wei. And now he would be her teacher. She could never have imagined that this was the beginning of her spiritual development, and the four years ahead would be a provision ground of sorts, setting Grace up for her spiritual unfoldment. But that is exactly what she was stepping into as she said goodbye to Michael Wei and made arrangements to attend his class when he visited the island next.

In later years, Grace wondered what would have happened if she had approached a Christian minister versed in the ways of the Holy Spirit. Would that person have affirmed her spiritual awakening as a work of the Holy Spirit? Looking at the call of God upon Grace, this spiritual event and subsequent pursuit of spiritual understanding and growth, was the first great pivot in her life to evoke spiritual transformation. Acts of the Holy Spirit invariably have salvific impetus, a saving grace behind them. This so-called chi awakening, a providential intervention, was indeed a saving grace. And it placed Grace firmly on her path of spiritual unfoldment and growth, *sealed with the Holy Spirit of promise.*

# 17

# The Eastern Way

Grace had said goodbye to her family in Adelaide and had journeyed west into her new life. The Island was closer to Indonesia than to mainland Australia. It was a four hour plane ride from Perth, Western Australia in a propeller plane that in high winds was blown side to side. This led the passengers to clap and congratulate the pilot upon successful landing.

Grace arrived in July of 1996 as the island began to dry out from its rainy season. She was surprised to find the island so small, at only fourteen by nineteen kilometres. It took no time to drive the length and width of the island, though much of it was rainforest and inaccessible.

The population reflected the size and remoteness of the island at just under fifteen hundred people, made up of expats from mainland Australia, and Chinese Buddhists and Malay Muslims from Malaysia. There was a rich blend of all communities on the island, a melting pot of diversity and acceptance.

Grace had been blessed by a friend who recommended her first for the job on the island, and then because he was leaving, suggested that she have his single flat. Most people shared very basic apartments. Grace was, even then, a solitary person, and well suited to living alone. It was the perfect forerunner to a small hermitage.

Her downstairs apartment was the size of a large walk in wardrobe. It had room for a single bed, a small wooden table and chair, shower cubicle and toilet, a bar fridge and single hotplate. A rusted, noisy, air conditioner protruded into the room. Electricity was free for resort employees. There was no telephone, no television, and wifi had not been invented. The end of the room where the cooking station was situated remained untouched from the previous resident, and Grace left it alone for two years, covered in spider webs and unapproachable. She ate at the resort or at the local Chinese Club. It was a lonely existence at first, but God sent her a message.

One day as she was walking up from the bottom of the settlement on a particularly hot day, her thoughts were looping escape. She'd been on the island three weeks. It was so culturally different, so sparse in everything familiar and so absent of family and friends that Grace wanted to flee.

Struggling to breathe, sweat causing her clothing to cling, she'd all but given up on the side of that hill, when a car drove alongside her. A man she'd never met, lent over and said, 'I'm the island taxi, hop in.'

Usually, Grace would never hitch-hike, but exhausted as she was and knowing the island population so small, she climbed into the front seat of the car. The driver looked at Grace's downcast state and asked her thoughts. Grace conveyed her desperation and desire to leave the island.

The man simply said, 'Give it three months.'

Grace looked at him. 'Three months.' He repeated. 'Every thing will change in that time.'

Well, Grace thanked the man for the ride once they were at the top, and she took his words with her. Later that evening when she told the women she dined with about him, they both looked puzzled.

'There is no taxi on the island.'

Grace gave a silent thanks to her Good Samaritan.

*Truly I tell you, there is no one who has left house or wife or brothers or parents or children for the sake of the kingdom of God who will not get back very much more in this age and in the age to come eternal life.*

Determined to give island life the three months, Grace eagerly joined the local Chinese-Malaysian badminton players for their spirited matches. The sound of the shuttlecock hitting the racquets echoed through the air, accompanied by the joyful laughter and banter of her newfound friends. Their skilled movements on the court kept her on her toes, challenging her to improve her own game and adapt to their lightning-fast reflexes. And the banquets afterwards made her feel welcome and accepted, despite being the only 'long-nose' in the club.

Master Wei came to the island as he said he would, a week after Grace's encounter with the Samaritan. He held qigong classes next door to the badminton hall and ran a Chinese medical clinic a few doors down. *Sifu,* 四福, Cantonese for Master, gently but enthusiastically encouraged Grace to participate in both the qigong class and the clinic. A steady rhythm of work and spiritual practice was developing, and then Grace received news from home.

It was December 1996, just over four months after Grace had left Adelaide, and her darling grandfather, Donald died. Fluid on the heart and stroke complications were attributed to an old injury he sustained in the prisoner of war camp. Not expected to live beyond twenty one years, he survived fifty two years longer than anticipated. But what number can be placed upon love?

Grace had mailed him a birthday card that week with a poem: 'My special Father-Grand'.

Donald departed for Home before reading it.

The father of the clan had gone. Agnes and the family were bereft. Nancy and John held each other and cried into one another's shoulders. Donald was the gentle, funny, solid and fair patriarch, one part of the foundation upon which many lives stood and grew. And now he was gone.

Grace didn't go back for the funeral but returned at the end of January. She was alarmed to see the grief in her grandmother.

Sunken eyes and a gaze that looked through things rather than at anything told Grace her grandmother was still in the shock of her beloved's death. A light had been snuffed and grief hung in the air in the Gleeson home like decaying petals left too long to rot.

Yet despite the cloud of sorrow upon the family, there was also joy. Melody had birthed her second child, a baby girl just two years older than her darling little brother. Grace's sister had checked herself and the baby out of the maternity ward and journeyed across the other side of the city to the hospital where her grandpa lay. There, she introduced him to his beautiful great granddaughter. Donald passed away the next day.

Grace stayed with her grandma for a few days. It was difficult walking into her grandparents' home without her grandpa sitting in his usual chair. No familiar music played on the record player. No laughter rang out from his storytelling. No quiet displays of love between he and Agnes. Unshed tears held at bay by her determination not to cry in front of her grieving grandmother. However Grace felt, she knew it was nothing compared to the loss her grandma was feeling.

Grace watched Agnes routinely go about the small, ground floor, single bedroom home. Her hospitality prevailed even when her granddaughter offered to cook or tidy or do some of the other small jobs. Agnes kept herself busy. Grace wanted so desperately to take away her pain though she recognised that the pain was a mirror to the love her grandparents shared. It was not for Grace to come between that union.

When it came time to leave, Grace realised that she actually wanted to return to the island, to embrace the offerings it was gifting her. The mysterious taxi driver had been right. The island had become a spiritual sanctuary of sorts, and she felt grateful for it. Leaving her grandmother was a tug on Grace's heart. The only consolation was knowing she was surrounded by loving family.

Upon settling back into island life, Grace's days were filled with a blend of serenity and activity. In the early mornings, she would join Sifu in his Chinese medical surgery. The scent of medicinal herbs lingered in the air as she watched him meticulously prepare his acupuncture needles and herbal remedies. The rhythmic kneading of his hands during foot massages created a soothing ambiance that resonated with the healing energy that flowed through the space.

Over time, Grace learnt the meridian points on feet and joined the team of Chinese practitioners who offered locals remedial foot massage. She became Sifu's assistant in acupuncture and soon learnt which needles were needed for specific ailments and where they would be inserted. Grace was amazed at the effectiveness of the acupuncture, and delighted in seeing people's limbs freed up and pain reduced significantly.

Outside of her spiritual pursuits, Grace worked at the island resort, marvelling at the strange atmosphere of the place. Despite its cheerfulness, and general business, Grace often felt a sense of emptiness. The excessive wealth that flowed through the resort seemed hollow, lacking the depth and meaning she yearned for.

And the night life of socialising and drink wore her down in her spirit. Truly, there was a war between her wounded worldly self that craved human companionship and acceptance, and her spiritual self that meditated each day alone, practiced qigong and sought a deepening of interior life.

Only her time with Sifu and the Chinese community satisfied this spiritual hunger. He was an incredible teacher and practitioner, and had certain abilities through the chi. Grace sat next to him over lunch one day and watched as he took a spoon to demonstrate chi in movement, and with the flick of his wrist, bent the spoon head in half. Try as she might, Grace did not have the strength to return it to its former shape. He could be in a class of people and teaching directional chi, could stand four to five metres from a person and knock them backwards simply by the thrust of his hands in the air directing the life-force energy. And many times, Grace witnessed Sifu heal a person's ailments with a simple touch to a place on their body.

His command of the chi was only outdone by his humility. It was through his tender guidance, that Grace deepened her knowledge and experience of inner and outer healing chi and began to explore the Tao, while attending temple and Chinese Buddhist celebrations.

Intrigued by the ancient Chinese philosophy, she sought to align her life with the elusive concept of the Tao, the 'Way'. Guided by the words of Lao Tzu in the *Tao Te Ching*, Grace found herself immersed in a profound text that offered insights on how to harmonise with the natural flow of existence. Its verses resonated within her, awakening a deep longing to live in accordance with the effortless action known as Wu Wei. She yearned to embrace a spontaneous existence, surrendering the need to control or resist the unfolding events of life.

Nature had what Grace considered an innate wisdom and symbolism, filled with signs to guide a spiritual journey. She recognised the natural world as a blueprint for living a balanced and harmonious life.

Yin and Yang, the embodiment of duality, captured her attention as she delved into their intricate dance. Over two days, she painted a two-metre size yin-yang on her external apartment wall in gold and blue. Light and dark, hot and cold, masculine and feminine—these opposing forces held a mirror to the complexity of existence, reminding her of the interconnectedness and juxtaposition of all things.

As Grace ventured deeper into Taoist practice, she discovered the transformative power of meditation, breath work, and a deepening of the energy cultivation in qigong and tai chi. She learned to attune her body, mind, and spirit to the vital energy known as chi.

These practices became her gateway to physical well-being, mental clarity, and spiritual growth. With each mindful movement and each conscious breath, she felt a profound connection to the cosmic forces that permeated all aspects of life. And she had a community of practitioners to share this with in Master Wei's students.

Grace discovered the profound beauty of Taoist rituals and ceremonies, where reverence and devotion intertwined. Observing these sacred acts, she learnt about deities, ancestors, and the elemental forces of nature. The offerings, incense, and melodic chants were considered conduits for deepening connection to the sacred, while fostering a sense of unity with the divine. It was this unity that she began talking with Sifu about and which led to a profoundly impacting conversation they shared about love.

By God's grace, Sifu had a real and steadfast understanding of selfless love. He was charitable, kind, generous with his time and wisdom, and loving and compassionate beyond self-recognition or reward.

It was twilight and the two of them strolled from the clinic to the qigong centre for the evening's practice. As they walked down a lush forest path together, dirt and pebbles crackling underfoot, Sifu Wei asked Grace if she would consider apprenticing under him in the hospitals in China, and in other nations around the world. Grace stopped and just looked at him, her mind a whirl of thought, emotion leading the way.

The Master continued, 'Before you say, make decision, we talk about Big Love.'

'Big Love?' Grace asked.

'Yes. Big Love. This is different to personal love,' he said.

They stood facing each other now. Grace saw in his face a glow that set her heart alight. Not in a romantic sense, but in a way that she recognised as responsive to a light within her. Grace was experiencing God in her looking upon God in Michael Wei though she did not know that then.

Grace was curious. The warmth in her body resembled the impetus that set her on a path to pursue someone for romantic love. Yet, it had no propellent. Sifu was not emitting romantic interest. Unbeknownst to Grace in that moment, the older man was exhibiting selfless love for her. Selfless love is often mistaken for romantic love. Grace, despite being unaware of this, was cautious nonetheless.

She listened to her Sifu even as she watched familiar processes within her. She was far enough along in her meditative and self-understanding practice to notice the wounded child wanting control. If that happened, the child would throw out a hook in an attempt to ensnare the man for her own love needs. Grace observed this inner urge and as her mindfulness practice taught her, she felt the rising of the pattern before cutting it off completely.

Sifu appeared to have noticed everything that had transpired.

'Grace, dear Grace. Big Love is the love that we have for all humanity. It goes beyond self and our own desires. Do you understand?'

Grace pushed back the hurt child who felt she was being chastised, and nodded.

'Yes,' she said.

Cognitively, Grace understood what Michael was saying but it would be another twenty years before she truly lived his words.

He continued, 'When we are called to be healer for people or to teach, we must love them all. There are no favourites. And all are loved. Even those we may not agree with.'

Grace felt the truth of what her mentor was saying. She remained quiet but nodded. It resonated with how she actually preferred to be with people. She really did not want to love a single person in an intimate relationship. She wanted to love all people.

In later life, Grace would marvel at how remarkable God was to have brought her together with Sifu Wei who, though he was Chinese Buddhist, lived the second greatest commandment Jesus called believers to in loving each other as they would love themselves.

Sifu lent forward and kissed Grace on the forehead. 'Good,' he said.

Later that night as Grace sat by her bed, she considered Sifu's words and his offer of working together. Grace knew that his teachings and wisdom would live inside her always. In fact, she thought, the Big Love that she had experienced as part of her self was now alive in her in a new way. She would ever be grateful to Master Wei for his instruction and guidance, but was her destiny entwined with his and his work for the world? She was uncertain.

Grace meditated on Sifu's invitation. She wanted to clear her mind of the various hooks that the offer grasped to, including the allure of travel and all that was vanity. It felt an honour that someone of such stature should consider her worthy of being his apprentice. There would be a certain degree of notability involved.

This plucked at the royal and nobility ancestry that lay in Grace, and which Sister Pretension relished. Grace wanted free of vain glory and pride to make this important decision.

Letting herself become still in body and in mind, withdrawing attention upon any sensory experience, by focussing on the breath, Grace entered the meditative state. Taking Sifu's invitation with her, she let it rest, bobbing freely in the consciousness sphere. Without clutching it, but with it in awareness, she watched associated and non-associated thoughts and feelings arise. Excitement. Tenderness. Love. Joy. Wariness. Fear. Greed. Hunger. Distance. Concern. Pride. The sense of being trapped. A question. Is this for me?

She let the thought float alongside the invitation. The two positions touched, acknowledged one another, considered a future together, immediately identified their differences and divergences, noting a fundamental variance in their end goals. The invitation was towards healing of people. The question, 'Is this for me?' drew a larger response, an objective that involved healing yet did not stop at healing. Though Grace didn't have the language for it, the answer felt more global than Traditional Chinese Medicine. It felt like saving humanity rather than focussing on healing in itself.

That was it, Grace realised. Having eliminated the clutter of mind and ego, she came to the root truth that spoke of the rightness for her being, and for her service. As soon as she approached the dilemma from a service perspective, allowing this realisation to rise up in her, she was clear. The service she was called into was broader and higher than a single strand of healing that Traditional Chinese Medicine offered. She could not ignore this realisation, and therefore, could not accept Sifu Wei's invitation to apprentice with him.

Grace came out of her meditation feeling equal parts free, sad and excited. She knew there was a calling upon her life, and now with clear mind, she knew Chinese medicine was not that path. She wasn't sure just what that path was, but she knew she had to keep herself available for it when it arose.

To her sifu's disappointment, the next day in qigong class, Grace thanked him but declined the offer. The young woman noticed a flicker of emotion pass across his ordinarily smoothly calm face.

He knew what that meant. And likely knew it before Grace. There was no need to continue their friendship. They were heading in different directions.

Grace felt her heart ache at the moment of this understanding. He would have taken her into his family, and shared his vast knowledge with her. It would have been a privileged position in Chinese medicine, but Grace knew in her heart that it was not the position for her.

Less than three months later, Master Michael Tem Foo Wei left the island for the last time. He handed the Traditional Chinese Medical clinic over to one of his older female students, and ceased all classes. Grace met him before he departed, handing him a gift of a charcoal drawing she had pencilled illustrating the beauty and serenity of one of the popular coves.

He smiled. It was a tender moment.

Grace's eyes filled with unspilled tears.

'You are a good person, Grace. Thank you for being my friend,' Master Wei said as he drew closer to her.

Leaning in, the wise man took his former protege's head in his hands and kissed her lightly on the forehead.

'Good bye Grace.'

That was the last Grace saw of the man who began her spiritual journey, and who introduced her to the values and concepts of the Tao, of Buddhism and specifically of the Big Love for all of humanity.

Michael Wei was God's gift to Grace, beginning her on her path to Christ through his own Christ-like nature.

Twenty years later and Michael Wei remembered Grace still. Unexpectedly, he telephoned to talk with her but she out so he left a message.

'Grace, this is Michael Wei, you remember me? Please call me.'

Grace's heart warmed to hear his voice. And yet, it feared as well. By then she lived a life away from Buddhism and Taoist practice. She was fearful that he would not approve of who she was, and so she neglected to return his call.

During this time Grace was completing her Phd. She let the busyness of her research be the excuse she needed not to contact him immediately. Then, as the distance of time grew from Master Wei's telephone message, Grace felt it too long a delay to call, though she thought of him often.

It was two years later, shamed by her disregard, when she finally sought him out. Telephoning the number he had left, Michael's wife answered. She gave Grace the sad news that her husband, Master Wei had died. It was a matter of weeks after he had called Grace. Michael Wei, knowing he was not long of this world, was ringing to say goodbye. Grace's heart receded. She sagged in her chair, an inaudible sob filling the vacuum of a crevice this news had punched in her chest.

'I'm so sorry,' she said. And hung up.

Grace was sad and aggrieved with herself. Even then her Master Wei taught our dear Grace about the value of honest and enduring friendship. Only after coming to Christ was she able to seek forgiveness and tenderly reach for her Sifu in heaven with words of love and blessing.

# 18

# Betrayal

Now, Grace had been on the island two years, and with Sifu in China, she had no teacher or guide. Spiritually aimless, between purpose, she slipped into a relationship with a man eight years her senior, George McGregor. George was a handsome Englishman with Irish grandparents. He retained a Mancunian accent despite having lived outside of Manchester most of his adult life. Tall with striking black hair and electric blue eyes, George was quietly confident, strong of opinion, athletic yet seemingly gentle with a kind manner and sensitive side that Grace appreciated. From the initial spark between them, the couple appeared happy though George did not share Grace's spiritual interests. They had been dating now for over a year and had come away to Adelaide for a holiday together.

Grace introduced George to her family who all thought he was charming. He took her to his parents' house where she met his sister, and mother and father. Everyone got on well though there was an air of 'something' that Grace could not quite put her finger on in the room as they sipped tea and chatted. Grace peripherally noticed their unease, catching pointed looks between George's father and himself, but she let it go in the light of she and George being in love. They explored the coastline and markets, and visited galleries with his sister, and any thought of ill-ease disappeared. The couple began talking about marriage and children, and their knowing of one another deepened towards this end. Or so Grace thought.

*The human mind plans the way but the Lord directs the steps.*

She and George had not been home a month when Grace awoke one morning in a panic. A voice resounded in her waking mind.

*What about Egypt?*

It was clear and authoritative. She had no idea what it meant, but in that moment, it felt like a warning; a severe warning as if it was imperative that she remain free of family obligation. Her only connection with Egypt was an interest as a teenager in the pyramids, but she hadn't thought of that for many years. And now that she and George were planning a life together, here came this foreboding.

Was it God? Was it the devil? Was it merely her own fears? Grace had no way of knowing. She was not versed in prayer. She had no notion of calling on Jesus or looking into the Word of God for comfort and clarification. She had no mentor or spiritual director to take this alarming pronouncement to for understanding.

Grace used her own judgement, which said with every fibre of her being that she could not have a child with this man.

She didn't tell George about the word she'd received. Grace simply said she didn't want a baby. He agreed, all too easily it seemed to her at the time. And so the prophetic dream of a decade earlier came true. She would never have another opportunity to mother a child. And while this was the right decision, the choice not to have a baby then was a grief Grace lived with for many years, until Christ healed and redeemed it all.

Two weeks later, the revelation of Grace's waking disturbance came to light. Unbeknownst to her, upon their return from Adelaide, George had planned a transfer from the island to another resort.

Now, as they sat with the manager of their department eating breakfast, Tony congratulated George. Grace asked what the occasion was and Tony, slapping George on the shoulder, declared, 'Egypt! What a great opportunity. I might even join you!'

Grace's head began to spin.

'Yeah, what a promotion.' Tony continued, 'You know, it'll be roasting, but the Dead Sea, wow! That'll be…'

At that moment, George caught his friend's eye and Tony abruptly stopped speaking.

'Oh, I, oh I'm sorry. I didn't realise.' And to George he added. 'You haven't told her?'

George shook his head.

'I'm so sorry Grace.'

Tony lay his cutlery down, placed his hand on Grace's arm, wiped his mouth with his napkin, and excused himself. Leaving his meal unfinished, Tony left the table, shaking his head at George before walking away.

'Egypt.' Grace said more to herself than anyone. The waking admonition repeated itself in her thoughts. *What about Egypt*, the voice had declared.

'Egypt? You're going to Egypt?'

'I was going to tell you,' George replied. 'Just waiting for the right time.'

'What about us? When were you going to tell me?'

Grace was angry and confused.

'I, ah, I would have told you.'

'When? Before or after you left?'

He looked down at his plate again.

'When do you leave?'

'Two weeks.'

'Two weeks?!'

'Yeah, I'll send for you when I get there.'

'What? We haven't even talked about it.'

'Don't you want to come?'

'I don't know. I haven't had a chance to think about it.'

Grace had a life on the island. She had friends, secure employment. She was saving money. Could she leave it all behind? Her thoughts were all over the place.

If he loves me why does it feel like he is sneaking away, she thought.

George saw the wavering in her face.

'I'll send for you once I'm settled.' He tried to reassure her.

'I guess so.' She smiled. Things were better when they agreed, Grace determined. She avoided confrontation and detested arguing.

'Good, good,' George said, 'Now, let's just enjoy these last weeks here.'

Grace nodded. It was all a bit much, and something didn't feel right about the urgency in George's voice. Still, she loved the man. They had seriously talked about marriage. Thinking to herself, she asked, Why wouldn't I follow him to a new life together?

Heaven had the answer to that question. And a ministry of unveiling ensued to help Grace find her own answer. Egypt and Grace would come together, but not like this and not now with George. God had other plans.

The next week was George's farewell celebration. As they were leaving the event, he began accusing Grace of ruining his night. George had spent the entire evening with his back turned to her, fawning over a young attractive new employee whose dress revealed an exaggerated cleavage. At one point they were laughing so loud, and sitting so close, Grace pulled him aside to suggest he might like to ease up on the alcohol. He had started drinking before they arrived at the gathering and was now quite intoxicated. George ignored her, and the attempts of Tony who subtly tried to separate his friend from the unseemly attentions of the young woman. Grace withdrew and to most present, it was obvious she was upset. George blamed her for bringing the party down.

When it came time to leave, they walked astride one another down the rear exit stairs into the car park. Grace responded to George's accusations that it wasn't her behaviour that was inappropriate, but she didn't get to finish her sentence. From the corner of her eye she saw a movement too late. George's fist smashed into the side of Grace's face. The force of the punch pushed her head into a nearby support beam. Grace's brain bounced from one side of her skull to the other. She was concussed. Blood poured into her left eye. She stumbled, and went into blackness.

Grace awoke the next morning in the small flat. She had no memory of getting home. The throbbing ache in her head and the inability to open her left eye brought back the evening's end. Like so many victims of partner violence before her and since, Grace searched for what she must have done wrong to deserve such treatment. She was remorseful. George came over and started crying when he saw the damage his fist had done. Grace held his head to her shoulder and she apologised.

'It was my fault. I shouldn't have said…'. Grace could not remember what she had said. But it must have been terrible to have elicited such a violent response, she thought.

Less than five years later Grace would learn the pattern of violence through her psychology training and work in trauma counselling. She learnt about how the perpetrator of violence, whether physical, emotional, financial or verbal enters into a pattern of abuse. At first there is the apology after the incident, then there is a buy back of favour where they show the person kindness through words or works or gifts or small measures of freedom. This brings peace in the relationship until the next explosion when another episode of abuse occurs, followed by an apology, the buy back, short-term peace and so on.

Grace didn't know any of that then, and amidst George's apologies, like many, Grace felt sorry for him. She took the blame upon herself and determined to do better next time. After all, she could see how remorseful he was, or so she told herself.

George's tears showed Grace how sorry he was for his actions. His concern over the wound in her eye showed Grace just how much he cared, despite not suggesting she see a doctor. And Grace was adamant not to let this one incident ruin their relationship. She would still pack up her life and go to him in Egypt when he called for her. They would marry and build a home together.

The next day as Grace prepared dinner in George's apartment while he finalised paperwork at the resort, a letter came for him. It was Monday and he would leave the island on Wednesday so much of the apartment was already packed up. Grace had seen where George kept his letters, so she went to place this one with the pile. He hadn't packed those yet, and she'd tell him about it when he came home.

To this day Grace cannot say why she looked. But she did. Perhaps it was the memory of the letter that her father had made her hide from her mum all those years ago. Either way, a letter sat opened on the top of a large stack of letters, all in the same envelopes and bound by a rubber band. George's name and address were written in the flowing hand of a woman. It was date stamped a week ago. Grace hesitated for a bare moment. She ignored the sensibility that said the letter was private. Something compelling drew her to take it out and read it. Perhaps it was George's flirtatious behaviour of the night before.

She read the first line, 'Darling.'

The thought came to her, I should stop right here.

It was too late. Her eyes had skimmed the lines following that affectionate address. She darted through one sentence after another, horrified by words that jumped out at her.

Throwing the letter to the ground as if it had stung her, Grace's stomach convulsed. Bile rose in her throat. The letter was explicit. Intimately detailed. Recent. Signed, 'Your loving wife.'

The room began to spin. She thought she would fall, but was frozen. Shock.

'Your loving wifc?' Gracc said aloud.

Gingerly picking up the letter again, she checked to see if she'd made a mistake. There it was, in all its erotic detail, a declaration unmistakable. Her partner of fourteen months was married.

Grace's mind whirled. But I met his parents. His sister. His friends. Tony! Does Tony know? No one had told her.

In the letter Grace had read, George's wife wrote that she was looking forward to seeing him in Egypt. She told him how much she'd missed him, and about all the things she would do to him when she met him. The intimacies of marriage.

Grace felt sick. She had not read all the letter. It felt too personal, too private, but she'd read enough to know she had been betrayed.

Grace cried out loud. 'We were going to get married.'

Emotions fought for dominance. Shame. Relief. Disbelief. Anger rose suddenly, pushing all aside. A tsunami of rage broke upon the shores of self pity. Slumped. Broken. Unaware of time. Grace walked to the toilet and vomited.

She felt empty. In shock. She tidied the letter back in its place among the other twenty or so envelopes, and bound them together again. Grace left the others unread. What she'd learnt was enough.

Grace left the half cooked dinner and walked back to her apartment in the Chinese quarter. It was rainy season and she let the thundering pellets soak her as her legs and feet mechanically moved one step after the other. Numb. Her clothes clung to her saturated body as she blindly, routinely, made her way through the streets to the residence area on the upper hillside.

Inside her flat it was quiet. There were no mobile phones. There was no television. Nor any visitors. Grace remained there that evening. George did not come looking. The next morning, the day before George was to leave the island for Egypt, Grace felt clear enough to go and see him.

Remarkably, he denied everything. Astoundingly, when she gave details of the letter, he said he was going to tell her.

'Before or after we had our baby? Before or after we planned our wedding? This is what Egypt is about, isn't it? You have no intention of me joining you! You're escaping this mess you created!' Grace's bruised eye hurt with the emotion.

He looked at the floor.

'No, no. I do. I want you to come. I would have divorced her.'

'That's not what the letter indicates.'

George started yelling that she should never have read his personal mail.

Grace walked out.

The next day George left for Egypt.

Grace didn't go to the airport. George didn't send for her. And they never saw each other again.

19

# A Message of Hope

George's betrayal crumpled our dear Grace. She felt like a fool. She felt dirty and ashamed. She wondered if the wife knew. If he beat her too.

Perhaps that's why he works away from home, she thought.

Maybe he knows his propensity for violence and can only do distance relationships. Grace's thoughts went around and around. She could barely focus at work. She learnt that while he lived and worked away his wife cared for their home in Brisbane, a two day plane trip from the island. She had visited him once on the island but that was before Grace had arrived.

Trying to understand the betrayal, Grace called his sister and confronted her. She spoke with his friends as well. They all said they'd advised him to tell Grace the truth, but none of them had told her directly. So much pain could have been avoided if truth had prevailed instead of deceit and lies. Grace's errant heart had already repented loving a married man in her younger years. She would never have entered a similar relationship again. The irony did not escape her.

Having ceased her meditation and qigong activities because George was more interested in golf, and without spiritual support from her Sifu, Grace turned to alcohol again. She worked her shifts at the resort and drank and kept shallow company, while daily questioning the morality of her life. Grace was stuck and alone. She was riddled with shame and had no vehicle for repentance or forgiveness.

Then, at a particularly low point, Grace was walking from where the resort bus dropped staff back past the Chinese food and games house, towards her flat, when she was stopped in the street. A young Asian woman, trotting down the steps to the lower street level, called to her before coming to a halt in front of the downcast woman.

'Grace?', she enquired.

'Yes', Grace didn't know the woman's name but she recognised her as a member of the resort's hospitality staff. She briefly wondered what the girl wanted to talk with her about.

'I have a message for you, from your aunty.'

Grace was delighted. She loved her Aunty Anne very much. Anne was her Uncle Jim's second wife. She was kind and insightful. They were a close family, and Grace loved them both and her cousins dearly.

'Oh that's lovely. Thank you Chen.'

The work tag hanging from the young woman's shirt let Grace speak to her by name.

'Yes. She says, "Don't worry. I look after you. I will guide you".'

Grace was perplexed. She hadn't yet told any family about the terrible turn of events with George. Too ashamed to even mention it to them, she was waiting for what she considered was the right time.

Grace was silent a moment. The girl continued.

'That is good. Yes? Your aunty, she looks after you'.

'Yes. Thank you. That's lovely. But, where did you meet her?'

It was Chen's turn to look puzzled. As if Grace should know, she said, 'In church.'

'In church?' Now Grace began to think Chen had the wrong person. As far as she knew, Aunty Anne had never been in a church outside of her wedding day.

'Um, I think you've got the wrong person.'

'No, no.' Chen insisted. 'I was just on holiday, and your aunty she come up to me and tell me, "You live on the island. You know Grace? The only Grace on the island." I told her "yes", and she give me this message. I said I give to you.'

True enough. Grace was the only person by that name on the island.

'What did she look like?' Grace asked.

'She is darker skin, eyes brown. Wears dress like a Sister.'

'What?'

'A Sister. A nun.'

'No', Grace almost laughed. 'No, Aunty Anne is blonde, blonde, blonde. Long hair, almost white. Blue eyes, skinny. Very pretty. Smokes like a train. And definitely not wearing a habit.'

Chen's eyebrows furrowed.

'What church in Adelaide was it?'

'No. I go home to Perth to my Church. Catolic.'

'Perth?!' Grace exclaimed.

The Western Australian city was a five hour plane ride to Adelaide where Grace's family resided.

'I don't have any relatives in Perth, Chen. This message really can't be for me.'

'Yes. Yes it is. She say, "Grace with long dark hair and glasses. Only Grace on island." You are the only Grace on the island. It's for you. She is caring for you.'

Grace could not deny that it fit her description, but she could not explain the strangeness of the message. A nun had approached Chen at a Catholic Church service and told her to pass on a message to Grace that she would be all right. More so, the nun was looking out for her, and would guide her.

Grace was mystified. Chen was confused but adamant. Grace thanked her, and they went their separate ways.

As she continued walking Grace realised that however strange the message was, it had given her comfort. She felt a little lighter.

Some months later, Grace saw Chen on the same piece of road just returning from another trip to Perth. Approaching her, Grace was curious to see if Chen had gone to church.

'Oh yes', she said. 'I want to tell that Sister that I deliver the message, but she was gone.'

'Oh?' Grace raised her eyebrows, waiting for more.

'Was very strange. No one knew who she was, only her name, Mary. Sister Mary. She was never at the Church before and only because someone was sick she came to replace. No one knows what church she came from or where she went. She stayed one day and then gone.'

Grace went very still. From somewhere within her, a prayer line she did not know she knew rose up…*Hail Mary full of Grace…*

'Mary', Grace all but whispered.

She and Chen looked at each other in the eyes, longer than the average glance. Both women smiled.

'Thank you Chen. Thank you.'

The younger woman seemed to be thinking the same as Grace. Knowing that her role in this heavenly mercy was now complete, she bowed her head slightly and went on her way.

'Mary', Grace repeated as she stood fixed. A vivid memory of her teenage dream came forward in mind. Mary's hand in Grace's as she led her towards the light. The Mother of God looking down at Grace saying, 'It will be a long journey, and it will be painful, but it will be worth it!'

Everything she had been shown in that dream had come true. A baby held out to her then gone. The man's betrayal. His violence. Death of a sorts in that the future she thought she would have in marriage was now gone. And Mary taking her hand, leading her towards the light.

Grace wept. Mary was with her still. Looking after her. Guiding her.

That was the day our darling Grace gave up alcohol, men, and meat. She returned to Buddhism and engaged telephone support with an Australian therapist. She immersed herself more deeply in the Eastern traditions, meditating daily and embracing a path of self-knowing, self-mastery, and self-emptiness.

# 20

# Buddhism

Grace immersed herself into the core teachings of Buddhism in the Four Noble Truths. The First Noble Truth, which spoke to her on a profound level, revealed that suffering was an inherent part of existence. This notion prompted Grace to reflect on her life, and to recognise how much time she had spent pursuing temporary measures to alleviate internal suffering. This awareness was a breakthrough that created a yearning in her for a deeper understanding of the nature of that suffering.

It became clear to Grace that the origin of suffering, the Second Noble Truth, related to a person's cravings, attachments, and lack of awareness or ignorance. She knew this in her alcohol consumption, and in the broken ways she pursued unhealthy relationships or found herself taken advantage of in relationships. With newfound clarity, Grace understood the need to let go of her desire for external validation, love, and acceptance. True happiness, she agreed, lay in overcoming those wounded drives and cultivating inner peace.

Reading the dharma, the Buddhist teachings, filled Grace with hope. She had observed her patterned behaviour before, and the recurring thoughts that made her feel awful, but was helpless to change them. Liberation from such suffering, according to the Third Noble Truth of Buddhism was not just a distant dream but was an attainable reality. By releasing her attachments and relinquishing her cravings, she could experience a profound sense of peace and contentment. This revelation filled her with renewed purpose and determination to steer clear of that which brought difficulty and suffering into her life.

It was reading and meditating on the Third Noble Truth that led Grace to cease drinking alcohol, which acted against her self-control and best interest. She gave up dairy for the same reason as it made her physically sick, as did meat. Her intestinal system was shaped differently than usual and digestion was difficult. Though the taste of various foods was pleasant to her, the aftermath on her body and brain was horrid. Grace took up intermittent fasting to deepen her meditative practice, and to assist her digestive system. She remained plant-based for ethical reasons to do with the preservation of life, for the rest of her life.

It was during this meditation time on the Four Noble Truths that Grace first considered in earnest the celibate life. There was a clarity and purity about this decision that let her spiritual pursuit become her main focus.

Grace was taking up the Fourth Noble Truth that paved the way for the cessation of suffering by confronting the root causes of that suffering: craving, attachment and ignorance. Through the relinquishing of those mental states and physical behaviours, Grace was freeing herself of a decade of patterned suffering.

She learnt that the cessation of suffering was not merely the absence of pain but a deep sense of liberation, freedom, and joy. It is the release from the limitations of ego, the dissolution of the boundaries that separate individuals from the interconnectedness of all things. This realisation brought an important shift in perspective in Grace, allowing her to perceive the impermanent nature of her emotions and feelings. While Grace didn't entirely agree with the Buddhist notion of the transient nature of the self, with no innate or surviving soul, she did appreciate the nature of changing states.

This awareness meant that Grace, who had a propensity for despair at times, particularly during the menses, was able to remind herself that her moods would pass. The evidence of joy that returned a day, two days, a moment later, validated this way of thinking. A key had unlocked a door on helpless repetition of painful patterns and with her mindfulness practice, Grace was finally feeling some semblance of freedom.

Ultimately, the cessation of suffering according to the Buddhist approach was an ongoing process, a continuous cultivation of mindfulness, insight, and wisdom. It required dedicated effort and a deep commitment to self-transformation. By integrating the teachings of the Four Noble Truths and the Noble Eightfold Path into one's life, individuals can experience a profound transformation, finding liberation from suffering and cultivating a deep sense of peace and well-being. This was just what Grace wanted and needed at the time.

The pursuit of the Noble Eightfold Path of Right View, Right Intention, Right Speech, Right Action, Right Livelihood, Right Effort, Right Mindfulness and Right Concentration, promised Grace a transformative journey if she dedicated herself to living it.

With an open mind, she sought to understand the interconnectedness of all things and the impermanent nature of reality. Then one day after a particular practice, a seed of doubt entered Grace's adherence to Buddhism.

Preparing for meditation one afternoon, Grace sat in her room on her meditation cushion. She closed her eyes, let her body relax, her shoulders drop and she took her attention to her breath. Breathing in and breathing out. Breathing in and breathing out. Her breath became a steady rhythm, gently guiding her into stillness. With every breath she became more and more still, the world around her faded away, along with her sensory experience. No seeing. No hearing. No feeling. Just breathing in and breathing out. Thoughts came and went but Gracc did not follow them. Like a leaf on a stream she let them float by.

Grace's consciousness became expanded and she began to sense a shift within herself. The boundaries that defined her individual existence started to dissolve. Grace felt an exquisite sense of connection with everything around her. The air she breathed mingled effortlessly with the space around her, and her consciousness moved out to embrace the entirety of her surroundings.

Several minutes passed before the now familiar shift in her consciousness indicated the beginning of the meditative state. She noticed her thoughts, and let them go. Noticed places in her body that alerted her of their presence, and let them go. Noticed sounds beyond her room, and let them go. All the while, coming back to the breath. Breathing in and breathing out. Until Grace noticed the absence of noticing. The space between thought, between observing. And she let that awareness go too with the distance between noticing and the absence of noticing increasing until Grace was in a perfect state of *śūnyatā,* emptiness.

This state was not void or absent but was a vibrant emptiness pregnant with infinite possibilities. As her consciousness touched that oneness, concepts of 'self' and 'other' registered as illusion, replaced by a profound understanding of interdependence and non-duality. No separation existed. The definition of separation could not exist in a seamless, undivided whole.

Within this emptiness, a vast ocean of One Mind undulated in living activity, receiving Grace as her consciousness came within proximity of it. Boundaries that had once defined her existence began to blur and fade. Soon there would be no Grace Gleeson, only the pool of unity that was the One.

Gradually, gradually…

And then, from within the whole the meditator, for a split second, registered herself meditating, even as she identified herself as Grace Gleeson about to dissolve into a single pool of consciousness.

As Grace merged with the vast ocean of oneness in that state of dissolution, she suddenly had a feeling—and that feeling was fear.

Confronting the impermanence of self, and the insubstantial nature of her personal identity was too much. She felt vulnerable, a loss of control, and in that moment truly feared annihilation of everything that was Grace.

Snapping her eyes open, Grace let out a long sigh. That was the last time she actively explored those emptiness states to that depth.

Dissolution of self was not the answer, she decided. She knew without knowing how she knew that eventually self would re-emerge, personality triumphant beyond the vast oneness. There was no need to go into that dissolution. After all, she had heard the voice of the One in her teens, telling her it was not time. There in that space, she was surrounded by personalities, living as they were beyond the physical realm of existence. They had not dissolved into the vast oneness of mind. And neither would she.

Instead, Grace continued her meditative practice but focussed more on mindfulness. She was still interested in Buddhism, having gravitated towards Tibetan Buddhism, but wanted to know what lay beyond the notion of śūnyatā. This was a practice, but it was only one part of a life dedicated to the Buddhist path. Grace set out to learn more about Dzogchen and Zen Buddhism, while continuing her qigong practice and maintaining her awareness of all that she'd learnt from Master Wei in relation to health and wellbeing from a Traditional Chinese Medical perspective.

As she was leaving the island, four years after arriving, Grace made a new friend, Harry. Harry was a good man, born of an Egyptian Jewish mother and a British father, already deceased. He was a practising vegetarian Buddhist. They clicked and remained friends for life. He married a Chinese woman and they had twins, a beautiful boy and girl. But before he found the love for him and settled down with a family, he and Grace set out upon a Buddhist pilgrimage together.

They worked backwards, beginning in southeast Asia and then onto China. From China they spent time in Nepal, and then many months travelling in India. They finally ended up in McLeod Ganj, a neighbourhood named after one of the British Lieutenant Governors of Punjab in the nineteenth century, Sir Donard Friell McLeod. The area had become home to the Tibetan population and government in exile.

Grace had hopes of seeking out a local healer there. Her qigong practice had been continual, and by sending the chi to any place in her body, she circulated it through the meridian points, the nervous system, the organs and throughout the body and brain. The only place Grace was unable to move the chi was through her heart centre where the energy would stick. She would not force it and it would not flow.

It made sense to Grace that this would be the place of blockage. How many times had her heart been broken. Still, it was essential for her longevity and ongoing health that she clear the wound to permit the flow to be smooth and regular. Grace knew that such blockages could cause serious damage to a body, causing all manner of entry points for future health issues and disease. She was determined to heal her heart before it was too late.

After one Indian man who'd set himself up as an energy healer, made an inappropriate pass at her, Grace refused to see anyone else. Her hopes of heart healing remained unsatisfied until she gave her heart to Christ, he who *heals the brokenhearted and binds up their wounds.*

It was now November 1997 and Grace and Harry had been in India for almost four months. Grace was tired. Exhausted. And then she got sick. Her temperature raged and plummeted. She was covered in welts and chicken-pox like pimples all over her body. Harry called the Australian embassy and they were prepared to send a helicopter to transfer her to New Delhi Hospital. And then back to Australia. They could fly in using the Dalai Lama's helicopter pad the following day but would await Harry's confirmation.

Miraculously, Grace's fever broke, and by the next day she had begun to stabilise. Two days later, she could stand. Over the week, she began to eat and drink more fluids, and was able to hold them down. Over the fortnight, the spots began to fade, and three weeks later, though still weak, she got the all clear from the attending pharmacist and was strong enough to respond to news that the Dalai Lama was now in residence. He would be meeting locals and tourists.

Harry and Grace queued for two hours in the blazing heat, Harry frequently insisting Grace drink and sit to rest. He was a good friend. As the time came for them to approach the Dalai Lama, Grace became aware of a peace that pervaded the area. She felt it within her. The man emitted peace. More than that, he seemed to Grace to be the centre of love. It flowed all about her. Her Sifu was a gentle man, quiet and humble, and displayed great kindness, as well as strength of presence in the chi. Here now though, the Dalai Lama was a living representation of that Big Love that Master Wei had taught Grace some four years earlier. She looked around and saw upon all the faces of visitors and attendants that they too felt the love.

When it was her time to meet the Dalai Lama, Grace bowed and offered up her kata. The white scarf was taken by an attendant, and as the spiritual leader of Tibet nodded receipt of the gift he encouraged Grace to take ahold of his outstretched hand. It was lithe, cool and soft to touch. For that briefest of moments, Grace felt herself an extension of the oasis of peace and love that was his presence. It was transforming. As if in the space of several heartbeats his very being offered her direct dharma transmission, something in her awakened. In that moment the true nature of her being was realised: love.

Though he held her hand, he looked at Harry whose six foot

three stature and shaved head gave the impression of a Western monk. He looked at Harry for a long time while he remained holding Grace's hand, as someone else tied a red string—the protection and blessing cord—around her wrist.

Dalai Lama tied a knot in it and blew the power of his mantra over it. Grace knew that she had received something beyond conceptual reality. She felt it alive in the nuance of her mind, without thoughts attached to it or images or even emotion. It was quite simply that something new was stimulated to emerge.

Grace didn't have long to wait to learn what that new thing was. After leaving Dalai Lama's residence she sat upon a mud brick wall in the heights of McLeod Ganj while Harry went to purchase more water. Despite the sweltering heat, Grace felt an inexplicable chill, hinting at a resurgence of fever.

Without interest, simply sitting in the after-experience of the Dalai Lama's field of influence, she watched three village women across the dirt track from her genuflecting. Full body prostrations on the ground, lying out legs and feet and arms and hands above the head. Up and down again. These older women, in their pinafore dresses and ancient bones, stretching out in prayer. It was then, through the haze of blurred and tired perception that the Dalai Lama's transmission realised its eventuality dissolving the gap between Grace's mind and the Spirit of God in her.

As she looked on, mid-prostration, with her own body wearily slumped, a voice cut into her mindlessness. It resounded into the space that the spiritual leader's transmission of true nature had created. The voice was one Grace recognised from her teenage heavenly experience. It belonged to One so filled with love, beyond human and even Big Love, as to be considered Love Itself.

That voice said, 'Everything you need is within you.'

And in that moment, a light went on in Grace. It was time to leave. Buddhism was not her way.

She and Harry booked a flight home to Australia the next day. He went to work in Singapore where he met his wife Jing. Grace entered university that summer and spent the next ten years studying and practising psychology and counselling. Her life was now dedicated to knowing how humans think and behave, and why. She wanted to alleviate pain and suffering of the mind in people through the psychologies and therapeutic interventions of the western therapy techniques.

She still practised qigong, joining a class run by an older Chinese woman, Elizabeth Yu, and started regular tai chi classes. Her mindfulness practice continued, making her a better learner, more compassionate and more able to discern her own tricky propensities. The Taoist Way remained with her throughout her spiritual discoveries and transformations. She had absorbed the felt experience of discerning harmony in the natural world, and discord when the Way was not followed. This became a guiding faculty of Grace's life.

And always, there in the background was Jesus, patiently waiting for God's timing to reintroduce him into Grace's life.

21

# Virgin and Child

In the first year of her psychology studies, now thirty years old and at university as a mature age student, Grace was still meditating daily but no longer studying the dharma. Despite this, it was now, some three months after her brief meeting with the Dalai Lama, that Grace experienced the full śūnyatā of emptiness, intraconnectedness, and the dissolution of illusory boundaries as she dissolved into the clear light mind without fear.

Grace was walking down Rundle Mall towards Adelaide University. It had been raining. Many people moved in multiple directions. Grace had come from a tai chi class. Her thoughts were on the quiet things of the mystery of life. She noticed as they shifted into dreamlike nature, a dissociative consciousness drawing her aware self back into itself. Her thoughts and sensations began to slow and dissolve. From farther back in awareness she noticed her consciousness shift, expand, open.

Momentum quietened itself. Time slowed. And then stopped. Everything had ceased to move. People in mid-step, mid-conversation, mid-laugh, mid-turn, mid-flick of the hair. Water in the fountain, mid-air, seagulls mid-flight, wings down or up, still. The fabric of the world ceased turning. To Grace, it became empty, yet, exposed in its aliveness.

In this clear light mind, Grace understood that before her, the world was empty, and therefore able to be created. Boundaries of self and constructs of identity softened in her perception of intraconnected life. All creation bound together by the very fact of being created by a Creator. And, where 'inter' implied separate objects coming together; 'intra' meant there was no separation. Within this, Grace also recognised the transient nature of reality and the illusory nature of labels, judgments, and divisions.

Looking on from behind the veil of interrupted motion the unseen, Uncreated Light touched Grace from within and she, now united with it, knew each person, saw the connecting features of human with human, felt their breath suspended, knew their desires, purpose, lostness, their obliviousness and their everydayness. She loved each child and each adult. Grace knew herself in them. And the light she perceived in them. There was no need to bring them into her heart, they were already there. Such joy. God letting creature perceive creature made God. In every person she saw a being of divine potential, able to become Godlike now and into eternity.

Revelation. The moment Grace understood this, that unseen hold on matter released. Noise and bustling people resumed. And she stood still. Looking at them all. Loving them all. Changed. Still young and immature in her understanding, but given by God's grace the transfiguring experience of the Uncreated Light that elevates a person's spirituality, and acts out its own momentum within a person.

Now something had changed for Grace. She lived in the world and observed it at the same time. She loved on the world and its people, experienced the mundaneness of life with all its suffering and emotional highs and lows, got caught in the machinations of wounded behaviours and others' woundedness and expectations, and at times looked on as a spectator in a theatre. Through the lens of the Buddha-mind everything was connected, nothing had intrinsic value in and of itself, and attachment to the world was illusion born of grasping mind. Her Taoist learning revealed the patterned nature of empty connection and let her be sensitive to the flow and harmony of the natural world.

Life at this time for Grace was a pleasant mix of study, painting art, tai chi, family and friends. It was a quiet life and amidst her psychology studies she had plenty of room to consider the mystery of life. Frequently, she would take her pondering to the art gallery next to the university. There, she would sit before a most magnificent rendition of baby Jesus in the arms of his mother, Mary.

For long periods of time, Grace would sit before William Bouguereau's painting, *Virgin and Child.* She knew grief. She knew loss. She knew sin though she did not know the word. She knew confusion, survival and compartmentalism. And she knew that when she sat with Mary and her small child whose eyes pierced through to her very soul, she was seen. Though the painting defied the clear light experience, it nevertheless came to life before her gaze.

*From heaven the Lord looks down and sees all humankind.*

Grace felt that the one who looked at her from beyond that painting, knew her and loved her. And she was forgiven.

*Those who look to him are radiant, and their faces shall never be ashamed.*

That painting heard so many confessions. All of Grace's stories. All of her woes; the decisions she could not make or did not know where to begin making. It listened to every one of her joys and her longings, her uncertainties and doubts. And there was no judgement there; in Mary was only a mother's love as she put forward the glory of her infant son who even in his nakedness held such resolute power that Grace wanted to fall to her knees on the ground weeping for his glory.

And she did weep. Before she knew about salvation in the Christian sense, that icon saved her. Not once, but many times. In a real sense, it was her refuge. There, Grace let God reemerge in her. And as she opened herself to possibilities, the Spirit of God within her was able to be more present. As her mind was less clouded, less busy, less self directed, Grace began to experience a felt impression of God. And she wanted to learn more about this love, for assuredly, the bubble of warmth she had felt as a child in church all those years ago, was now present again.

And as God does, it was not long before she was led to *Sophia*, a Dominican convent and round centre for groups, of which Jungians were a part. Grace had been interested in the works of Carl Jung since being on the island. Having read his memoir, *Memories, Dreams, Reflections,* Grace felt finally she had met someone who spoke her language. She now underwent personal weekly therapy with a Jungian analyst, who was a Sister of Saint James, with a view to becoming a depth analyst herself.

When she and her girlfriend, Hannah, a beautiful soul of a Christian woman who had been a missionary when younger, went to London for six months in 2002, Grace attended the weekly Faye Pye Grass Root Seminars in the C.G. Jung Club.

They took a side trip to Switzerland, and Grace relished the experience of visiting Jung's house and the Jung institute there where she wanted to study. This was not to be. God had other plans for our Grace, but now back in Adelaide, she delighted in partaking of Jung lectures at Sophia, and speaking with the Dominican Sisters who lived in the convent on the property.

The Sisters befriended Grace, and even purchased a number of her paintings to decorate the Sophia building. Grace felt herself akin to them. Not quite the same, a little apart. She longed to experience community as they did, and the love they seemed to share in a holy life. Still, there was part of Grace that held back, feeling herself called in a different way for a purpose beyond what was before her.

One day, as Grace sat opposite one of Sophia's leaders, Sister Mercy, she described the bubble of warmth and this feeling of God to the nun. Listening to the young woman's description of the majesty of her felt experience of God, the older Sister's voice quavered a little.

Her eyes welled up as she said, 'Child, you are so very fortunate; many of us long for such experience.'

Grace knew then that the Dominicans were not for her.

She went back to her painting in the art gallery, and poured her love into that child, despite at times feeling fearful. Grace would look into his piercing blue eyes for any sign of condemnation, certain she deserved it.

Every now and then the devil would tell her, 'There! See that! A judgement! He does not love you anymore. How could he. All that you have done.'

But Grace would be drawn to the extraordinary gaze of his mother, looking down at her child, so confident in the knowing of his specialness and what he was offering the onlooker. So resolute and fixed in his majesty. And when Grace would brave looking back into the eyes of her beloved Jesus, because that is what he had become once more, beloved, she saw so much more than a baby sitting on the knee.

Grace saw kindness, forgiveness, an offering unlike other infants who have their own needs. This baby's outstretched arms offered to pick her up, to take her into his arms; to cover her with his salvation. In those moments, that tiny pink light of flesh, arms open, eyes fixed on hers, became Grace's sanctuary and refuge.

Yes, that icon ignited in Grace a fervour of faith. It upheld a belief in her of the presence of Jesus in the world and his active ministry in her life. There in that art gallery, seeds planted by God decades earlier were being fertilised, no matter if it all just now remained a mystery to her. *Virgin and Child* was a saving grace, a gift of God, from the One who knew what would be coming next in our darling's life.

22

# Mysteries and Secrets

Now, in all of creation, there are many secrets and mysteries. Great heavenly glories will forever remain withheld from people—secrets known only to God. *For my thoughts are not your thoughts, nor are your ways my ways, says the Lord.*

Mysteries and secrets are part of God's divine plan, a reflection of God's infinite wisdom and love. For many, God is a mystery to be discovered. And God, who knows each person, the intimate details of the hidden desires of the heart, the unspoken prayers whispered in the stillness of the night, wants to be discovered; wants to be found. And all a person has to do is trust that wisdom and trust that love.

Trusting in God's will requires patience and faith. It often involves waiting for God's timing for revelations or understanding that certain secrets may never be fully disclosed; earthly or heavenly, but that an eternal heavenly goodness imbues it all.

For *the human mind plans the way, but the Lord directs the steps.* The trust that a person has in God's plan leads to personal growth and spiritual transformation, even in difficult situations; even when what is a mystery turns out not to be a mystery at all but a well kept secret. And this is exactly what our darling Grace is about to learn.

By now, Grace knew secrets and she appreciated the mysteries of creation. And by God's grace, our darling trusted that her life had a divine hand behind it; that she was known to 'the Universe' and therefore any unknown factors of her life would be shared according to the mandates of that goodness. Of this, Grace was certain. And it was this certainty that helped her through the coming season of discovery. So too, she would eventually recognise that her own belief and trust in what she came to know as God's plan was a gift itself. She came to understand that even her certainty was carefully orchestrated over the course of her life.

Divine leadings not only instilled trust in her but enabled Grace to accept God's timing and call on her. This providential care was to become increasingly apparent as a symphony of souls gathered to perform a most majestic composition of heavenly magnitude under the greatest Maestro of all, for which Grace would ever be changed.

23

# 'I Wanted To Tell You'

On the 3rd of July, 2006 Grace learnt the truth about the great mystery of her life, which was in fact a great secret; a truth held by a few people not including her. The sense that Grace had of being different, of being treated differently in the family, would very soon be understood.

It was time. Indeed, in order for God's plan to unfold, the plan made for Grace's life, as it is uniquely laid out for each person's life according to their given circumstance, Grace needed to know certain details of her life. Details that caused her to experience growing up, family and love as a mystery. A mystery 'out there', unsolvable, unfathomable, uncertain. Details that shaped every aspect of her life from friendships to relationships, education and career choices, to how she perceived and felt the human condition, to how she felt about herself, and how she was set apart from her family. The secret that was to Grace the great mystery of her parents' behaviour towards her, and towards each other when referring to their daughter, was now ready to be released.

On this winter's evening, Grace had invited her mother to stay that weekend in her two-bedroom unit. She thought it would be a lovely opportunity for them to share some mother-daughter time. In all the years Grace had lived out of the family home, over twenty years now, Nancy had never stayed with her eldest daughter though they had often talked about how nice it would be.

The arrangements of that evening were the portfolio of a select group of beings whose designation remain unknown, but whose remarkable feat of bringing mother and daughter together, set the scene for a momentous shift in the lives of a single cluster of human beings within one family. The ripples of that evening continue to effect the thoughts, decisions and consequences of persons in that family, and will do so for another generation yet. By the very nature of Grace's experience, her story presses into the lives of many more around the world. Its values, its example, releases in those predisposed towards the truth of their own God-seeking, and promotes the position of heavenly interest up the rank of their life pursuits.

Everything was arranged. With subtle angelic leading, no invasion of thought, Grace had turned the television onto a particular channel, not noticing its discussion of a contentious Australian law that had been passed over a decade earlier. About the two women, a heavenly ministry prepared to assist the unfolding of the next series of events. In fact, there was little for them to do once the scene had been set. Nancy and Grace naturally followed their own predilections based on their respective life experiences. They arrived at the exact place that any divinely orchestrated leading would have prompted them.

It was dark outside. Dinner had been shared. Curtains were drawn. Grace had the lamps on in the lounge room, creating a soft environment for the evening. The atmosphere was perfect for both mother and daughter to feel held. To feel safe.

Nancy was seated on the blue-grey sofa as the television sounded in the background. Grace was in and out of the lounge room getting bedding ready for the spare bed, having been at work that day and unable to prepare earlier. She walked in from the bedroom and saw her mother focussed on the television. Nancy was fixed to the screen.

Grace turned to look at what was so captivating of her attention. The programme became the catalyst for the night's events. Yes, everything had been planned well. A heavenly event on earth. The show was merely the vehicle used to introduce the night's topic into the room. Thoughts and words of the women would be their own.

Nancy remained looking at the television when she asked her daughter, 'What do you think about that?'

'Oh I agree with it. All those children who are now adults, who can know their parents. Yeah, very important.'

The women referred to Australia's policy of allowing adopted children to access their records, which identified their birth parents. Much debate surrounded the benefits or not of this decision for the child and both sets of parents.

'I don't know,' said Nancy, still not looking at her daughter. 'All the pain those poor mothers must have felt giving up their children. It's so long ago. Why dredge it all up again? And imagine how the parents who adopted the child must feel. I mean, they *are* the parents.'

'But what about the children mum?'

Grace had worked as a lead research assistant on a major university project that investigated the welfare of children in separated families. Should parents talk with their children about the separation? Most couples elected not to and the research found that children faired much better in the separation process when the parents had taken time to sit down with their young ones and share the plan of separation with them. Grace had come away from that project with a sense of how valuable honest communication is and a notion of child-centred practice in family relations.

For Grace, the child's welfare, for their childhood and their emotional growth into adulthood and wellbeing, was paramount. And it was the parents' responsibility to ensure their children's wellbeing remained uppermost in their decision-making plans and processes.

'Surely, they have the right to know who their parents are mum? Imagine having that part of them absent. Just not knowing must be so difficult. They'd already feel so different I reckon.'

'Perhaps it's best that the children don't know.' Nancy was still looking at the television.

Grace thought of the son of her good friend, Felicity, who was unaware that his father was not his birth father. The boy, Jason, had been raised by Franz, who had met Felicity when she was pregnant. Franz and Felicity were no longer married but Jason still considered Franz his father. Jason, then aged fifteen would fly to Germany, where Franz had returned to and remarried, and would spend several months of the year with his brothers and sisters of that marriage. He was unaware that there was no biological relationship between he and his father, or his father's other children.

On one visit, Jason had a sudden heart complaint during a skiing accident in Oberstdorf, Bavaria. Quick action by Franz sent the teenager to hospital where he recovered well. During that stay though, his bloods were taken. Jason was a rare AB negative blood type but neither of his known parents were a match. His unknown biological father must have passed that blood type onto him.

Both Jason's parents were relieved to learn that his heart condition was manageable and not life-threatening. They were also considerably relieved that their secret remained protected. Felicity was adamant that Jason not find out about his parentage. She had no way of tracking the birth father, and had no intention of telling her son about him.

This was one topic that Grace did not delve deeply into with her friend. She loved Felicity and valued their friendship more than the need to win her to what Grace considered was a morally wrong decision. She thought Jason should know the truth about his father, but it was not for her to decide.

'What about the medical side of things mum? It's a bit different, but you remember how distraught Felicity was when Jason had that heart scare.'

Nancy nodded.

'Imagine if he had needed a blood transfusion or organ transplant.' Grace knew this was highly unlikely but she was trying to get her point across.

'Or later in life he has some disease or something. He has no idea about a whole other side of his medical life, and Felicity won't tell him.'

'I don't know. I still don't think it's a good idea.' Nancy turned to look at her daughter.

Grace stood a metre away from her mother. They had always spoken honestly together. Later, Grace would reflect that perhaps they were honest about everything except this one thing. Perhaps honesty was what hovered around a secret her mother had kept for so many years. Indeed, perhaps honesty was what helped her mother maintain that secret.

Grace had kept her father's secrets from her mother, and her mother's financial secrets from her father. It hurt her to do so, and it hurt more when the other parent learnt that Grace had known. Each expressed a sense of betrayal by their daughter. Yes, Grace favoured parenting that put the child's welfare first. And she despised secrets.

Grace's trust in people was slowly eroded by secrets. She thought then for the first time in many years of the man she had loved and was going to have a child with, who was secretly already married. And secretly violent. Yes, Grace's trust had been broken by those secrets. She thought secrets were poison in the world. Destroyer of lives. Orchestrations of dark forces. And so it was from this history that our Grace argued for a child's right to know the truth of their parentage.

There she was, looking down at her mother as Nancy argued for why it might be necessary to withhold information from a child. Attending angels looked to the Spirit of God within Grace, and to the Spirit of God within Nancy. They evaluated the timing. God had already taken note of the potential harm and dismissed it according to the benefits it would bring to both women, and for God's glory as their lives unfolded according to God's plan. The time was right.

Without Grace being conscious of it, the Spirit of God in her drew nearer, touching her mind. Angels stirred the air and something unseen shifted in the space between the two women. For Grace, it seemed as if the air about her stirred. She had known such an impression when time stood still and the veil of mind gave way to śūnyatā and the clear light mind. But this was different. This shift occurred in the space between her and her mother as if reality was being reshaped even as they spoke.

Grace knew that conversations between people had a spatial dimension in the relationship as much as they had verbal and physical components. The space between individuals engaged in talk, moved and shaped itself around the spoken word, thoughts and behaviours of each person. The space between held vital information that could fill out the gaps in any conversation. And it often held the truth, just waiting for a moment to be released.

What Grace did not know then was that at times this spatial depository is administered by an angelic ministry or interceded by saintly administers of God's word, or by the Holy Spirit in person; that at times, there are hosts of unseen heavenly aids holding nuances of God's truth that in the exact right conditions can suddenly, yet gently, be released. And therein lies realisation. Epiphany. Revelation. Knowing beyond all science knowing. The space between persons is filled with the formerly unknowable now known.

Well, there in the space between Nancy and Grace, the conversation was no longer single layered. A second string of meaning was now attached to each sentence. The underlying melody of human words filled the room but with Nancy's last sentence a harmony had been added, where before it was not. A harmony so subtle, yet vibrationally tangible. Words within words. Enough of a change for Grace to notice. The top layer of conversation masked the layer beneath it; the layer that held an unspoken truth. That shift in the space that those words and their melody created was palpable to Grace.

In that moment, Grace's consciousness unexpectedly altered. With a clarity she could not explain, and a directness she had not anticipated or even considered, she looked her mother in the eyes. Before she was actually aware of it words sounded out of her mouth. It was as if she had rehearsed this moment all her life. Not verbally. But in feeling. In the undercurrent of her loneliness, her sense of rejection, of separation and longing, of seeking and of watching.

'If there's anything you need to tell me mum, now's the time.'

Grace heard herself. Heard her words. A laugh, not attached to those words, one that seemed to come from a far distant place, from her everydayness, prepared to make fun of the statement. Grace was about to make light of it and in the increment of the moment looked upon her mother expecting her to laugh at the same time.

Suspended, Grace's laugh did not manifest. And neither did Nancy's. Rather, her mother's face went pale before it reddened. Grace noted the contrast of her mother's skin against the material of the couch. Her blue eyes took on the hue of the fabric then brightened as tears began to well.

Angels stood back. The Spirit of God in both women touched each ever so slightly, pressing truth up above all else.

Grace looked at Nancy, somewhat puzzled. Why is she crying? What did I say that was so upsetting. Grace's mind scrambled to retrace what she'd said. She couldn't recall exactly. It already seemed so long ago.

Nancy was speaking now. But lost in her own thoughts, Grace missed the first few words. She need not have worried for they kept tumbling out of her mother over and over again. The same lines.

'I wanted to tell you. I did. I wanted to tell you.'

Grace deflected and cut off any sudden feeling she might have had. Alarmed at her mother's obvious pain, she softened her voice, as if speaking to a small, frightened child, and softly asked, 'You wanted to tell me what mum?'

Everyone in that room was now still. Not an angel moved. Not the unseen host who witnessed this revealing of human reality for divine purpose. Grace's whole body held itself. Contained. Vigilant. Evaluating. Breathing.

'What mum?' she asked again. 'What did you want to tell me?'

Nancy looked straight into her daughter's eyes, pleading, fearful.

'It's okay. You can tell me anything, you know that.'

Grace's training and counselling experience with people subjected to trauma came to the fore. She knew how delicate disclosure was, and how it could teeter on the precipice of truth revealing only to fall back into the land of perceived safety, remaining ever hidden and unrevealed. Slow and gentle was the key.

And then, Nancy spoke.

'Your dad,' she said.

'Yes? What is it. Is he okay?' Grace waited.

'Your dad. He's, he's not your dad. Well, he is your dad, but he's not your real dad.'

A heart beat. The room froze. Nancy looked at Grace whose eyes had dilated. She didn't know that her daughter had disappeared and reappeared within that heartbeat. Her voice was the same quiet, gentle tone as she'd used to invite her mother into truth.

'Dad is not my real dad?'

Nancy shook her head. 'I wanted to tell you.'

Grace continued to look at her mother waiting to see if she was joking. But the tears flowed down Nancy's cheeks. She looked at her daughter with such a mixture of emotion—fear, guilt, expectation—that Grace realised she was serious.

Shock cushioned the young woman. As the reality of her mother's words was unleashed within, Grace felt a punch to her stomach. A punch so hard she buckled over, at the same time as a voice within let out a stupendous, almost insane laugh. Within, she fell to the ground. Crushed.

To Nancy, none of that happened. Her daughter remained standing, unmoving, silent not three feet away from her. The older woman did not see the fluctuating horror, pity, relief or incredulity her daughter experienced. She did not notice the tumult of emotion or the dissociation Grace entered, followed immediately by numbness. Grace had very early on in life learnt the mastery of self-disguise. She played it supremely now. As if she had formerly only ever been practising for this moment.

Calmly, Grace walked through to the kitchen where she retrieved some tissues for her mother, put the kettle on and proceeded to make a cup of tea for the two of them. She had no words, and she wanted to remain quiet until this truth had landed fully within her. It was far from settled and Grace did not want a reactive emotion to escape her.

There and then, Grace felt the impact of Nancy's declaration but she had not fully absorbed it. That would take years. For now, as she stood in the kitchen, her mother's words swirled around her, floating about in the space between them, poking at the young woman, trying to enter her mind.

Grace felt nauseous.

Nancy had followed her daughter into the kitchen. Grace turned from the kettle and took in the sight of her mother. She looked wretched. Taking two steps forward, she folded her mother into her arms. Almost forty years of holding this secret poured out upon Grace's shoulder as Nancy sobbed and shook with the force of emotion.

The kettle whistled. Steam filled and moistened the air behind and about the two women. Grace observed this from a far off place. One hand resting on the rear of her mother's head, the other rubbing her back, Grace soothed Nancy while it seemed to her that the tiles on the kitchen floor rose up and swam in the air threatening to swallow her whole.

Motion sickness increased. Her consciousness was on the verge of shutting down. Too many words. Images. Too many memories. Too dizzy. But she and her mother stood there holding each other, propping each other up. Both needing reassurance that the other would not run away.

Grace closed her eyes as Nancy said over and over, 'I'm sorry, I'm sorry.'

And Grace, stroking her head and back repeated, 'It's okay, it's okay.'

Actually, it felt a long way from okay. The realisation that a distant and persistent knowing was now confirmed felt more surreal to Grace than anything she had experienced. Her history was unravelling. Someone had pulled a thread and the fabric of reality was slipping through her fingers.

My dad is not my dad. She thought. My dad is not my dad.

It was difficult to catch ahold of this reality. There and then gone. Her mind repeated, My dad is not my dad, trying it, tasting it, seeing if it fit with her known world. Her mind would register it then flick it away as absurd. Only Grace kept repeating it to herself.

My dad is not my dad.

Something inside her was so deeply hurt. A long silent scream, part disbelieving laugh, part self-pity, part excitement and relief for finally understanding why her life had seemed a lie, rose up in her as she struggled to remain conscious.

She stood alongside the news now as if viewing it from and about another person. She felt it necessary to gain distance there and then if she was to remain upright.

Dissociation. A mental process of disconnecting from thoughts, feelings, memories and sense of identity. Humans do this in daydream, in shock, in trauma, and when a parent tells their child a great portion of their life has been untrue.

Grace found it difficult to remain objective for long. Floods of memory, words, images from her past washed over her. And the thought recurring—

My dad is not my dad.

Grace gently let Nancy go and made them both a cup of tea. They sat down at the dining table that had once belonged to Donald and Agnes, and talked. Initially, Nancy was reticent to say much, but gradually she opened up.

She had been intimate with a sailor in 1967, become pregnant, and though Grace’s grandfather Donald had searched for the man, the man himself had given obscure details of his origins to Nancy, and her description of him matched someone else she knew. Donald never found him.

Instead, some months later Nancy met John Gleeson. He was an eighteen year old army soldier. That part was true. By that time though Grace was already growing in her mother’s womb. God already knew her. God already had plans in motion for her life.

Nancy did not want to marry just because she was pregnant. John was persistent and Nancy found herself falling in love. John knew the child she carried was not his, but this didn’t deter him. He was smitten. On the third proposal, Nancy said yes. And on the 2nd of December 1967 Nancy MacMilan married John Gleeson in New Zealand. Two months later, little Grace was born.

Over the ensuing days and weeks of her mother’s disclosure,

Grace had to situate the truth of her parentage in place of the stories that had been told to preserve the secret. Her identity unravelled. She had spent years conducting family research on the Gleeson side of her family. She had met cousins, second cousins, distant cousins on the Gleeson side. She had pursued historic stories and brought them into herself, owned them as her own. She had located long lost family members, great grandparents and great-greats, and great-great-greats. So many documents of lives, of records, marriages, deaths, legal papers, newspapers, hospital records, ports, ships, deportations, islands lived on, lives stolen and enslaved as convicts, then freed. Irish, English, Scottish, Indigenous, Indian and more.

All of these Grace had taken into her identity. Indeed, her university Honours thesis had been based on the search for Peter James Gleeson, her father's grandfather who was suspected to have had an Indigenous Australian mother. None of it hers. Her whole thesis was based on a lie. She was embarrassed. She felt like a fraud. And something else. A pain that had been soothed began to seep afresh.

The longing inside her, the difference she had felt from family and from the world, had been abated somewhat by ancestry research and the facts learnt about family members. She had begun to feel a semblance of belonging to a wider community of family. But they did not belong to her. They belonged to others.

When these thoughts came, Grace would find herself laughing out loud. She thought of her friend Felicity and her son Jason.

What on Earth? She would exclaim. And laugh again. Not the kind of joyful laugh a child has when giggling. More an ironic laugh.

I can’t believe it. Then she would catch herself and with a rueful smile think, Actually, that’s the thing, I can believe it.

At that, her head would get too light again and she had to forcibly cease the tirade of thoughts.

‘Why didn’t you tell me mum?’ Grace asked as they sat together at the kitchen dining table, cups of hot tea held between hands untouched.

‘Your dad was adamant. He made me swear. He thought you would think of him differently and feel that you weren’t his, but he’s always thought of you as his daughter.’

‘But it had the opposite effect mum. I always felt different. I never felt like he loved me or cared for me the same as the twins.’

Nancy’s hand reached across and took her daughter’s hand. Grace hurt. It was many years before she became angry. At those times, she would question how they could have kept the truth from her.

She had moments of spontaneous anger, mostly thinking about how different her relationships could have been. Grace always sought after a father figure. This led her into unsafe situations and into relations that compromised her values. She grieved her relationship history and the lack of fulfilment there, and felt cheated by the family secret.

Still, her anger did not last. She was too empathetic and too capable of understanding other's perspectives to hold to anger long. And she reasoned that even having known the truth she may have stumbled into similar dynamics of relationships the same.

That is the fact about human free will. No matter the divine plan set in place for each individual, a person is always free to choose a course of action. Invariably, those choices will be reactive responses to conditioned rearing and situational context.

It is rare for a person to choose the will of God in young years. Clouded judgements, outside influences, poor guidance, the masks and mirrors of society posing as helpful education and culture, traumatic experience, and the myriad subsequent emotions a person may have, all prevent or limit the presence of the indwelling Spirit of God from making inroads into the human mind and decision making.

Ceaselessly and tirelessly we are called by the Spirit within us to turn around, to know that God is there with us. How many errors of judgement, harmful experiences, downfalls and missed opportunities could be changed for better, if only humanity would lean into that presence within.

Grace did not know this yet, but she knew enough to know that life's decisions needed to disentangle from the patterns of conditioned behaviours and falsities told to a person in their young life.

Eventually, both mother and daughter went to bed, neither sleeping very well. Grace spent the night thinking about what that secret had brought into the family. How her father could not be himself. How he could not fully be a father; always checking himself to determine if he was treating the children the same.

What a secret to hold. How sad, and yet, how noble, she thought.

## 24

# 'I love You More'

In the days and weeks thereafter, it was this nobility that Grace chose to focus on after learning the truth. Her dad knew that she was not his biological daughter and yet he chose to marry her mother and to raise Grace as his own. Her heart swelled for him in those moments where true values stood out against her own heart. Those values of nobility, good and care were elevated in Grace's thoughts. She wondered what it had been like for him.

My dad, she thought. He is my dad, and will always be. He raised me, ensured I was fed, cared for, and grew me up. In so many ways, John Michael Gleeson offered God the greatest sacrifice of all. He gave his life.

Grace marvelled when she thought this way. How extraordinary was her dad. Still, every now and then she would awake from disrupted sleep as the voice of her hurt inner child cried out, Yes, but what about the truth!

Grace gave her mum a few days to tell her dad that his daughter knew the truth of their biological status. She was adamant that there be no more lies.

Nancy feared telling John, but her daughter insisted, 'Or else I will tell him. And I want the twins told as well. No more lies. No more secrets.'

In the family, only Nancy's parents, Grace's grandparents knew, and her mother's brother, Grace's Uncle Jim. Donald had been deceased for many years, but Agnes, Grace's grandmother, was still alive. So much made sense to Grace now.

How much easier it must have been, she thought, to send a toddler away to live with her grandparents when she was not really a part of the couple's growing family. A couple who were having children of their own. Grace finally understood so many anomalies in her childhood experience.

The first thing Grace did after Nancy had spoken with John, was approach her dad. Driving to her parents' house that day, Grace really didn't know what to expect. She and her mother had talked on the telephone. Nancy said John was angry with her for disclosing the secret. He was also concerned that Grace would no longer think of him as her dad.

Though there was a great whirlpool of emotion inside her, with memories jumbled and tumbling, all vying for their position of truth in the new paradigm of her being, one thing stuck out, one thing she knew for certain. Grace was grateful. Grace was filled with admiration and love for this man who took a baby on as his own. John Gleeson had an eternal place in Grace's life, and would not be discarded simply because they were not biologically related.

Grace entered her parents' house through the back door and greeted her mum as usual. They hugged and kissed and brought each other into an embrace. Nancy watched on as Grace approached John who was standing in the lounge room. Nancy was already in tears. John had backed up against the coffee table which was positioned in front of the lounge room window. He could not get any further away from Grace in that moment. But he couldn't move back anymore.

Grace ever remembered the look on her dad's face as she walked towards him. She had not seen it there before. Fear. As she moved closer, he lifted his hands in the air, palms forward signalling her to stay back.

To John, Nancy had betrayed him. How could she disclose this secret, their secret. He felt alone. His world too had now changed. Before he could torment himself further, Grace skipped a step forward and pulled him into an embrace.

This was unheard of in the family. Grace could not recall when her father had begun hugging his children or showing affection. It was a gradual process from brief body bounces, to one armed around the shoulders hug, to tickle hugs, and as grandchildren came along, to full body hugs. Because of the violence in his childhood shows of affection had not been learnt though the Spirit of God in him would attest that John Gleeson felt and loved deeply. At this time in their relationship, Grace and he were at the regular hug stage but not too long and not too often.

Gradually, John's arms enfolded Grace.

'I love you dad,' she said, her head nestled on his chest.

He mumbled something.

Grace leaned back enough to see his face.

'Truly.'

Grace felt she needed to press home to him all that she was feeling, to reassure him of the place he held in her heart. Still holding each other in embrace, looking directly into his shiny pale blue eyes, eyes that quivered with uncertainty, Grace said, 'Dad, I probably love you more now.'

A look of hope tinged with puzzlement came to his face.

'You chose to be my dad. You chose to raise me, to give me a home, to care for me. You didn't have to but you did. How could I not love you. I love you more for that.'

By this time, tears were falling from his eyes. His body relaxed. Grace was crying and she could hear her mother sobbing behind her.

Angels sang.

*And you will know truth, and the truth will set you free.*

Spirits of God in each of the three, mother, daughter, father, were united in joy.

Healing. Restoration. That is God's promise.

A week later, Nancy and John held a family gardening day. It had been planned for many weeks now. One of the bordering trees needed to come down as it had started to drop branches. Grace's brother and sister were there to help, as were their children. At Grace's behest, Nancy asked the twins, along with John, to step into one of the bedrooms. David and Melody looked concerned. Of course they would. Never had the family gathered like that before.

'We have something to say,' said Nancy.

Neither she or John had wanted to tell the twins, but Grace would not permit the lie to continue.

'It is not fair on them,' she had insisted.

She did not speak other thoughts that swam around in a mind still adjusting to her place in the family. Thoughts that spoke of her uncertainty.

I need to know if they will still love me given that I am now technically a step-sister. That is so weird. 'Step-sister'. No, I'll never use that term, she thought. I am there sister. But I need to know if they feel the same.

The twins looked from their mother to Grace, to their father. Grace was nervous. She felt dizzy and was sure she was trembling. Still, she would have spoken, but Nancy wanted to tell them. It was her story before it was Grace's, and God had chosen Nancy to be the truth teller.

In the end, Nancy just said it, plain and clear.

'Dad is not Grace's biological father.'

Both twins looked at Grace to see if she was going to laugh. The same reaction Grace had when Nancy told her. Grace was not laughing. John looked at the floor.

David disappeared. He stood still, but his eyes went vacant. Dissociated.

Melody cried out, 'I knew it! I knew it!'

David recovered and looked at Grace again trying to take it in.

Melody was excited.

Pain. Fear. Unwarranted shame. Grace had entered fright mode. Frozen. Eyes wide. Heaven's exactitude called down salty tears.

Nancy continued to speak while John stood still and silent.

'It doesn't change anything.' Nancy echoed Grace's own words to her dad. 'Grace is still dad's daughter, and she is still your sister.'

The twins nodded. Melody was still smiling though both she and David now had tears in their eyes.

'I hope you can still love me.' Grace almost begged.

Somewhere not far off, a gentle wave of heavenly mercy poured forth into the room. Everyone was now crying. The family came together then, hugging and sobbing. Nancy asked the twins not to tell their children just then, that over time it would be known.

This was Grace's concession. It took five years before all members of Grace's family were made aware of Grace's biological status. It changed nothing notable between them towards Grace.

Melody shared that she had always wondered. As the twins' children had aged, they too noticed differences between their parents and their Aunty Grace. Each of them began to ask questions.

'Why does Aunty Grace have brown eyes, and everyone else in the family have blue eyes?'

The fact that the twins were blonde and blue eyed only served to highlight the difference more. Children learnt the genetic passing on of eye colour at school. They were curious how one in the family could be different to what they had learnt. Prior to truth disclosure, and even after it, the adults became complicit in the lie. Family members struggled for answers to the questions or changed the topic, while Grace remained quiet.

When they were all told the truth, the five children from age fourteen to twenty-four were accepting of the news. Relating with their aunt continued as usual, though amongst the more sensitive of the children, Grace did notice a certain additional effort to include her in ways that might ordinarily have gone overlooked.

David had not suspected. He had never speculated Grace's biological standing in the family, and by his own admission, had not considered it possible. Whereas Melody had felt something different about Grace in the family. What was true for the twins was different for each of them, and different again for Grace.

That is what personal truth is: it is based on individual experience. And while truth can be a shared belief, it is made up then of multiple personal experiences of reality all agreeing on a single idea; an idea they agree to be true.

Divine truth is fundamentally and functionally distinct from worldly or intellectual truth. Divine truth has divine unification at its centre. It coordinates with worldly truth only in as much as the truth one endeavours to speak and live has the qualities that promote union with God. Truths fabricated for personal, political, ideological or religious gain that are clothed in falsehoods are the antithesis of divine truths. They are the error of humankind and serve to perpetuate a demise and separation from all that is divinely good and true.

Truth set Grace upon a new path. She had a few months to get used to the idea of the new family dynamic before she left. Having applied to various universities to complete a Doctorate of Philosophy, Grace was once again packing up her life. Now, she moved to Melbourne determined to start afresh.

The truth had set her free, and heavenly hosts made ready melodic notes from On High delighted to see what manner of life Grace would create for herself.

# 25

# Miracle Night

Over four years full time, Grace completed her Phd research in Melbourne in the psychologies of trauma. She was now 40 years old, and having graduated, declining academic roles, Grace worked part-time in community health, counselling those in emotional and psychological need, and pursuing her spiritual interests in her free time.

Grace meditated daily and had a keen interest in the unseen mystery of creation. Her spiritual hunger had drawn her towards the esoteric Celtic mystery traditions. She had joined a British based mystery school and was studying the Qabalah and meditating on the Hebrew letters each day. That month, her meditations were on the Hebrew letter Aleph. These daily observances had opened in her an inner quest for spiritual truth.

Grace yearned to know the facts behind creation, and the reality of the unexplained spiritual phenomena and psychic experiences that had been part of her life since she was a little girl. Studying the Qabalah afforded her the time and discipline it took to explore the inner nuances of her spiritual world. In that space of silence and depth, of layered meaning and close piercing into the fabric of the ineffable, Grace felt connected to something bigger than herself. While she did not think about it then, it was always the presence of her teenage experience with God that she sought.

Many years later, Grace came to realise that since feeling the all encompassing love and security of God, since hearing God's voice, she had been searching for it again, seeking out that union. And while her stance on God had softened a little, and her friendships included Christians, she was still an unbeliever who denied biblical notions of God. She now had a Bible, gifted to her by her mother but she did not read scripture. The Holy Book awaited the time when it would become her dear friend. For now Grace used it to store her special birthday cards or precious mementoes.

Now all of this was about to change, and the next increase in Grace's spiritual growth was about to unfold.

In the early hours of Wednesday 19 August 2008, Grace awakened suddenly, becoming aware that she was not alone in the room. She lay very still, then with great courage, opened her eyes. There, in front of her, Grace saw a young boy floating cross-legged in the air above her knees. He was fair haired and appeared about seven years old. He held out his right hand and looked down at several small, coloured orbs floating above his palm. Around the boy and through him, and through the orbs, glowed the most peaceful, powerful light. Grace was transfixed. Her entire being sank into peace, a peace more buoyant than salt water, more light than graciousness personified, and more radiant than the sun. Every fibre of her being gave into the sanctuary and acceptability of his presence.

The boy looked from the objects in his hand to Grace. An invitation for her to look into them. As they turned, seemingly unaided, not touching the luminescence of his hand, but seemingly part of the pattern of his radiance, beyond gravity, turning slowly, around and around an inch or so above his palm, the orbs seemed to glow a little brighter.

With no words spoken, Grace knew that if she looked into them she would receive a great treasure of personal revelation. She would be given a piece of the jigsaw of herself that she was not even aware was missing, but which was necessary to make her whole.

As she watched the small orbs float and rotate, Grace felt her spirit move, a little like the pressure and release a person experiences at take off in an aeroplane. Upon release, she was back in the hospital ward in Adelaide, where she had visited her grandmother only a few days before.

Grace watched herself rubbing cream into Agnes' heels where they were raw from the hospital sheets. She felt the tension in her grandmother's body ease, muscles loosen as a barely audible sigh signalled the relief of discomfort. In that moment, Grace became aware of her own outpouring of love. Every soothing touch, each turn of her hand over aged flesh and thin, raw skin, brought forth another wave of unconditional and unguarded love.

Grace watched herself glow as she tended to her grandmother. She observed the softened feature of her own face, the elegant movement of her hands and fingers that glided effortlessly. Such intimacy of care. A care of one who knows another. Of one whose life is given over to that other. Grace could have wept for the beauty of it as she witnessed herself and her grandmother.

And then, she was back in her Melbourne apartment, with the boy still hovering over her prone body in bed. Grace followed his gaze now to the centre of her heart and there she saw a cavity that went right through her.

Beyond the material realm, this hole opened up into a vast cosmos. Colours and swirls, stars and all manner of creation existed there in that space. Vast and magnificent. And alive.

As Grace marvelled at it, the deep love she had for her grandmother resonated within her. And into her mind, in that moment, she heard the angel say, 'Turn that love around and love your self so'.

And with those words, Grace felt a surging build-up of energy that rose and rose, and burst out from that cavity in her heart in the most brilliant white light. That light streamed out of her, even as the love nestled within her as a dear friend long absent. Grace knew in that moment that the journey of integration involved learning to love oneself. What she did not know then was that she had witnessed the Uncreated Light of God.

And as the understanding of Love dawned on her, the boy smiled ever so sweetly. A smile that encapsulated so much. Approval. Satisfaction. Tenderness. A mission complete. Grace looked at him with the greatest of awe.

Through his most beautiful smile, she heard in her mind, *Raphael.*

The angel's radiance and Grace's own light and glowing warmth were the last things she remembered of that night. The next thing she knew, it was daylight. There was no angel in her room. Everything was just as it had been when she went to bed – except that it was not. Everything had changed, because Grace was changed.

Grace leant over to her bedside table to take ahold of her journal. Her hand trembled slightly as she paused in mid air. She was different. She was new. Lighter. Glorified. Suddenly, and most profoundly, Grace knew God.

And a realisation struck her as if she had always known it. So profound in its truth and simplicity, Grace spoke its truth into the air.

'We are born to live that we may find our way home to God.'

And now, she would dedicate her life to this very thing - finding her way home to God.

## 26

# Follow Me

God was calling Grace, calling out her name, singing in her ears and in her mind and she was hearing but had until now, refused to listen. She was deaf to the call because the world and its offerings were louder, more accessible, more pushy and glitzy, fashionably, alternatively acceptable in the arenas of her life.

After so many years of deaf ears, eyes that would not see, and pain that was too loud and too present to let hope and faith and Jesus in, something changed for Grace.

God had sent an angel to her. Raphael.

*I am Raphael, one of the seven angels who stand ready and enter before the glory of the Lord.*

And that angel had shown her how to love herself. It had revealed to her the face of God within her heart—the sacred heart. And this revelation had erupted a spontaneous conversion to God.

*Blessed be God. May his great name be upon us, and blessed be all the angels throughout all the ages.*

Now, a matter of months later, the calling upon Grace to enter into all that God had planned for her, took another turn. Grace was suddenly and powerfully struck down on her right side. There was no accident, no injury, only pain severe enough to immobilise her, and where necessary demand she use a walking stick. Tests revealed no obvious trauma to the hip region. There was no medical explanation. It was as if all the pain of former years, all the heartache, betrayals, letdowns, abuses, grief, all gathered there in Grace's right side. She went from fit and able to limping and walking stick overnight. Doctors could not explain it; physiotherapists had no answers and pain medication did not resolve the issue.

Grace was now offering trauma workshops and counselling in community health. The pain in her hip became so debilitating that she could barely navigate her way to and from the health centre.

Grace despaired.

*Wait for the Lord; be strong, and let your heart take courage; wait for the Lord!*

And then a non practicing Catholic friend, Cara, whom Grace was working with in community health, mentioned the name of a physiotherapist who used acupuncture needles. With Grace's history of apprenticing with Michael Wei and seeing the remarkable healing capability of acupuncture, our dear Grace made an appointment.

It was her first visit. What would be her only visit. Grace lay on the therapy table in a room set aside for treatments in a private residential home in Melbourne's city area. She had just received manual treatment and now the therapist placed several acupuncture needles in Grace's body with one between her eyebrows. Grace closed her eyes as the woman left the room to let her patient rest in the acupuncture.

Silence. Grace had a good measure of relief in her hip. For the first time in months, she felt a semblance of relaxation though there was a persistent throbbing that remained.

Grace invited her whole body to relax. As she started to actively let muscles rest, a slow dawning occurred to her of a presence in the room. Her eyes were closed but she could sense someone at the end of the therapy table where she lay.

She must have come back in, Grace thought of the practitioner.

Thinking it was time to come to and finish the session, in a very relaxed and slow manner, Grace opened her eyes and stared down the length of the couch—

—into the face of Jesus.

Clothed in white, a robe of soft material, a rope around his waist, light radiating all around him, his arms out wide, he had the most loving smile, with mouth closed and lips slightly upturned.

And there in her mind she heard his voice, *Come. Come child. Come to me.*

Grace wanted nothing more than to throw herself into his arms, but she could only stare at him, silent tears leaking out the corners of her eyes.

*Come child.* He said again.

Grace smiled, and blinked, and he was gone.

When the physiotherapist came back into the room, Grace kept the experience to herself. She held it close to her heart. It was too precious to speak, too wondrous to breathe into the world.

Only when she met Cara later that day did she feel able to share her visit from Jesus.

'I had no words Cara. I couldn't move. I just lay there looking at him. O, he was so beautiful. So filled with light. What should I have done?'

Cara shrugged a little and took on a far off gaze into the distance.

'Probably nothing Gracie. Except give him your heart. You know that Bible passage in Matthew', she asked her friend who already shook her head, no.

'"Come to me, all you who are weary and are carrying heavy burdens, and I will give you rest." Maybe he just wanted you to have that rest darling.'

'Yes, that makes sense. As I looked at him, all I could do was what I had done as a child, and that was open my heart to his love, and to love him in return. And so I did Cara. I opened my heart and let all the love he was giving me live within me. O Cara, all I could do then was to love him back. I felt my heart so full.'

*We love because he first loved us.*

Tears welled up. Her friend leant over and took her hand. Sharing testimony was easy in that moment, with an empathetic, therapy trained, spiritual friend. Grace felt safe and heard and genuinely held as she shared this momentous gift.

As their time together drew to an end, Grace stood up to farewell her friend. She was three quarters the way to the apartment door when she noticed that her hip pain was gone, completely and irrevocably healed.

Grace did not experience that pain again and from that time on, Grace spoke with Jesus every day. She meditated and gave her thoughts to him. She asked him for guidance and took him her troubles. While she did not see him, she talked with him nonetheless, sharing her innermost hopes and dreams.

Grace didn't know she was praying. She wasn't aware of the many, many ways a person can pray and seek spiritual counsel. There was no formal knowing in her about worship, steeping in God or soaking in the Holy Spirit or being born again or having Jesus enter her heart. She knew none of this religiosity. Grace simply had a private love between herself and Jesus. And oh, how she loved him and was now so utterly aware of his love for her.

Yes, there were times when she doubted. Times when the doubt was so thick in her throat and mind that she thought herself deluded. Why would Jesus come to her? There were times when the plethora of new age concepts overwhelmed her so that she actually lost his name.

On top of that, Grace was embarrassed to share with others the love she had for Jesus and the relationship she was quietly cultivating with him. Ashamed she was unworthy of his magnificence and kindness in her life, it was easier to turn to alternative philosophies and ideas than have to face what she felt sure would be Christian condemnation. Though she did not realise it, this was the remnant of a young girl being met with the rhetoric of sin in her first Church encounter. Such was the enduring effect of that conflicting time.

Grace had no role model for one who had given their heart to Jesus. Her only Christian friend, Cara, turned to Buddhism. Grace struggled. She walked in and out of churches hoping that someone would see the earnest seeking within her. She sought out Catholic nuns to sit with, to talk to and confess to. They heard her and released her, marvelled at her, and at times conveyed envy for the love of Christ they witnessed in her. But they were not enough to help Grace hold to Jesus' hand, to aid her in bringing him permanently into her heart, and into his fold.

That would come later when Grace had finally rid herself of the many masters and distractions.

Praise God, who is *abounding in steadfast love and faithfulness, forgiving iniquity and transgression and sin*, that his Holy Son Jesus knows his own, even as his own know him.

And glory be to God that Jesus' mercy and salvation mission is available to all peoples of God's creation: *I have other sheep that do not belong to this fold. I must bring them also, and they will listen to my voice. So there will be one flock, one shepherd.*

Still, much had changed in Grace's life. Even her clients had changed. Now, many of them brought spiritual dilemmas to her. Something marvellous was happening within Grace and in her life. The two were converging, for the first time. Her spiritual interior began to be mirrored in her external life.

One morning while meditating and talking with God, Grace had confided in God, 'I want to serve.'

And he had answered, 'You have served, and now you will serve in earnest.'

*Like good stewards of the manifold grace of God, serve one another with whatever gift each of you has received. Whoever speaks must do so as one speaking the very words of God; whoever serves must do so with the strength that God supplies, so that God may be glorified in all things through Jesus Christ.*

After God's word to her, Grace found herself in situations where she was invited to share her love of Jesus with friends and clients when they indicated an openness to receive that love. One friend in particular, Michelle, who was also studying the Qabalah, was so moved by Grace's testimony as to explore her faith more fully. She too eventually let go of all other voices and followed Christ into his Church. Michelle went on to serve as a minister in the very same church that Grace had attended as a child. Her message of the Gospel contained all the compassion and righteousness of Christ's own ministry. Yes, Grace's world was changing. The light of Christ was permeating her life more and more.

Then, quite unexpectedly, in an ordinary morning's meditation, Grace heard that now familiar voice of the Spirit of God within her say, 'And now we move. Our work is here.'

And a flash of Great Britain appeared in her mind's eye.

# 27

# To Be Near You

The year was now 2012 and our Grace was forty-four years old. She had just graduated with an award-winning Phd, and was stepping into the next chapter of her life.

She had taken her mother home to Scotland the year before, with one of Nancy's oldest friends, Charmaine. Nancy and Charmaine shared a particular history in that they were together on the night Nancy met Grace's biological father. Still, as many questions as Grace had, Charmaine had fewer answers. No one knew anything about the man, and Grace decided to let the idea of ever finding him go.

She was on a mission. She'd had the word from God. Their work together was in the United Kingdom, and she was preparing to visit Britain for a conference with the Qabalah school in which she was now supervising students. This would be a reconnaissance trip to discern God's word on their relocation plans.

Agnes, Grace's darling grandma, was now ninety-three years old. Forty-one years had passed since she stopped her Tiny, her adored granddaughter from walking out beyond Park Road driveway, 'To go to him'. They had shared a remarkable friendship. Grace had continued to stay at her house while she lived independently. It made her feel close to her grandfather as well. And she knew how much her grandmother missed him.

Theirs was a beautiful love, one of those marriages where the flame of youth's love is still evident though deepened and matured with age. The specialness of their relationship impressed itself upon Grace even as a young person. Her grandmother often spoke about how Donald was waiting for her, and that they would be together again.

When Grace stayed with Agnes, before her grandmother went to live with Grace's uncle Jim, she would hear the older woman talking to her beloved before she went to sleep. Agnes would stand in front of a photograph portrait of Donald as a young man in uniform. Grace didn't listen in to her grandmother's words, but she could feel from their tone, they were of love. Agnes would simply smile at her granddaughter when she climbed into the bed that they shared, her words and love treasured up in her heart.

Here Grace was now, in Adelaide, saying cheerio to her family before going on a six week holiday to Britain to attend the workshop and to determine what God wanted of her.

Agnes and she sat parked overlooking the water. Moana Beach

was their favourite place to visit. The whole family spent hot summer days at this beach when Agnes and Donald first migrated to Australia. It was now seventeen years since Donald had died. On one of their drives, Grace asked her grandmother if she still missed him. Agnes replied, 'Every day. I miss him every day.'

Now Grace and her grandmother sat in the car sharing hot chips and ice-cream, occasionally throwing out a chip to the flock of eagerly awaiting, squawking seagulls. Agnes grew up by the sea in her hometown of Peterhead in Aberdeenshire. She giggled like a little girl at the gulls' delight.

As conversation moved towards Grace's holiday, Agnes mentioned the old black and white photograph of Grace as a toddler leaving Park Road house.

'Ever since you were tiny, you had a suitcase in your hands.' She smiled.

Grace thought there was a hint of sadness in her voice.

O how she loved her grandmother. Every time they were together they'd talk about all manner of things. Grace would ask her about her life, about Scotland and nursing, the war, her family, her brothers and sister, and about her beliefs. There was no deception in her grandmother. She was polite and would often reserve her preference to appease the majority, but she was not evasive or untruthful or secretive. If she didn't want to speak about something she would say it was too private or too sore or she didn't know the answer, but mostly Agnes delighted in intellectual and philosophical discussions, and enjoyed reminiscing. O and she had a rich sense of humour. Without being pretentious, Agnes also knew the finer things of life. She had an old worldly etiquette about her with a modern sensibility that meant she could speak to current affairs. She taught Grace this etiquette and had passed it on to her daughter Nancy.

This propriety didn't stop either of them supporting Grace unconditionally in whatever direction she felt called to go. In fact, the entire family always loved and championed their dear Grace wherever she was led.

Driving away from the beach now towards Nancy and John's, they passed their favourite view of the coastline of Port Noarlunga. A memory of one of their first visits to this lookout washed over Grace. Agnes could still walk freely then. Grandmother and granddaughter stepped out of the car to look from the heights of the clifftop out along the long majestic turquoise coastline, ocean meeting sand. Holding their recently purchased double scoop ice-cream cones, no sooner had Agnes closed the car door than a gust of wind came up the cliffside, blowing her ice-cream clean off the cone, and splatting against her pretty mauve woollen coat. Well, the two women laughed and laughed.

Now, Grace slowed the car as the view drifted in sight. She took a long breath in and shared what was on her heart.

'Grandma?' She waited for Agnes to look at her. 'I know about dad. I know he's not really my dad, well, my biological dad.'

Now while Agnes loved Grace fiercely, she was rarely

voluntarily tactile. She hugged and cuddled, but it was not often that she touched people. There in the car, Agnes reached across and took Grace's hand.

'Yes,' she said. Nancy had told her mother that Grace knew the truth.

As Grace continued to drive with the one hand steering, Agnes continued.

'He *is* your dad Grace. You've always been your dad's wee girl.'

She went to lengths to reassure Grace that John loved her, something Grace had struggled to believe most of her life.

And then she looked at her granddaughter and smiling sweetly said, 'He must have been a good man.'

And that was all Agnes said about Grace's biological father, but she spoke then about the old black and white photograph. Her grandmother was convinced that a supernatural imperative had moved Grace towards searching for a father 'out there' whom the toddler had not met and did not consciously know existed. She believed that even as a baby, Grace had felt him missing, and had taken it upon herself to go and find him. Both women retired in thought wondering how a two and a half year old could know such a thing

Could divine leadings begin so early? Are they so personal to a person, so individually specific? Grace concluded that they did start early and that they were uniquely personal to each soul. She imagined that some innate guidance system, placed there by God, was active in her at that young age. A long ago impetus set her on a trajectory to locate her biological father, and in so doing to find her way home to her Heavenly Father, to God, even if it only expressed itself as something humanly missing. Grace marvelled at her God and the provision made for her in her life.

After a brief visit with her parents, Grace drove her grandmother home to her son's house. She made sure she was sitting comfortable in her chair, her tartan blanket across her knees, a cup of tea on the table next to her. Weak black with a splash of water. And then she bent down and kissed her grandma 'tattiebogle', Scots for goodbye. The kind of goodbye that isn't permanent, but a short farewell for we'll meet again soon.

The two women looked at each other. Fifty years between them. Agnes's eyes were now milky pale blue. Despite the cataracts that she had always refused to have treated, her eyes twinkled. Her softly lined face was smooth, creamy, without a hint of the sun's brush. She retained her Scottish complexion. Laughter lines spoke of a joyful life.

She grasped for Grace's hands. Her granddaughter could feel the emotion of time welling up in her. This was it. They both knew it. Agnes would be gone when Grace returned from Britain.

There was nothing left unsaid between them. They loved completely. A protective love. A love without blemish. Never once a harsh word. A full, eternal love.

Hands resisted letting go. The longest they'd ever touched. Grace kissed her grandmother's cheeks again.

'I love you grandma.'

'I love you too, Tiny darling.'

Grace knew she had to leave. Her uncle and his wife and eldest son were giving them space, but were in the room. Grace was aware that she needed to leave before she broke down.

With her grandmother's chair facing towards the rear of the house, Grace let her hand go and walked towards the front door. She reached the hallway and ran back. Taking her grandmother's face in her hands, she smothered her in kisses. The older woman giggled as kisses caressed her forehead, cheeks, lips, nose, chin and around again, over and over.

'I love you so much grandma. It's so hard to leave. You know that right? I'll see you again. I will.'

'I know Tiny, I know. Go now darling. I love you.'

And Grace walked to her car and cried all the way back to her parents' house. In her heart of hearts she knew, and was aware that her grandmother knew, this was their last meeting before heaven.

And so it was. Grace was forever grateful that she had made the trip from Melbourne to Adelaide to farewell her grandmother before flying to Britain.

Grace was in Manchester. It was Mother's Day. While she knew God now, she was still not part of God's Church though she felt a call to minister. To that end, Grace was counting on the boat that would row her across the hemispheric divide from Australia to Britain to the Interfaith Seminary in England. There, she would train as an Interfaith Minister. Perhaps, she thought, that would give God the best opportunity to lead her to where Jesus needed her to be.

It was May 10th, 2012, Grace had attended the introductory session about Interfaith Ministry. Yes, this would be the first step in her journey north, and it would give her a story to tell people instead of the one held in her heart. That story knew that God had plans for her. She doubted it was in interfaith, but all she had was her faith that all would be well. That story the people in her life would not understand.

So there she was having attended the mystery school workshop that week, and now the interfaith seminar. She was part way through lunch at a local vegan cafe when a text came through from her mum.

'Grandma isn't well. It's not looking good sweetheart. She's in the hospital. I'll call later.'

It was the early hours of the morning in Adelaide on the other side of the world. Agnes had rung the bell on her bedside table to awaken her son, Jim.  He found her sitting up on the side of her bed.

'Jim, make me some tatties and a cup of tea will you, and then take me to the hospital. It's time.'

Agnes resisted going to the hospital when she was unwell. For her to ask now told her son that she was seriously unwell and knew it. He made her potatoes and tea and because she wouldn't take an ambulance, drove her the forty minute drive to the hospital.

It was evening now in Manchester. Grace reached out to friends and received a prayer to pray for her grandmother to be healed, even if that meant gently letting go of her worldly life and physical pain, to enter into eternal splendour.

A few hours later, God gave Grace the discernment that Agnes' spirit had returned to the One who made it.

And so it was that evening, in the early hours of the morning in Adelaide that Grace's darling grandmother shed her mortal body.

Grace did not need to be told. She knew.

A text message came through from her mother, 'She's gone, Tiny.'

Nancy asked Grace to call in the morning. She had just lost her mum and couldn't speak just then.

Grace wept. She cried her heart out. A part of her was grateful that her grandma was now at peace, no longer in pain. Another part was bereft. What would the world look like without her grandmother in it. She couldn't imagine.

*My joy is gone, grief is upon me, my heart is sick within me.*

Her friend Tom, whom she'd met at the weekend workshop and who lived in Edinburgh, called for a chat, not knowing about Agnes' passing. He simply said he felt the need to call. For over an hour, Tom listened to Grace speak about the woman who was her second mother. He patiently let her weep, be quiet at times, sob and laugh with storytelling. God's great mercy sent her an earthly servant at her time of need. When they came to say farewell, Grace was feeling a little more steady.

*Blessed are those who mourn, for they will be comforted.*

Night had drawn in on her hotel in Manchester. Exhausted, she fell quickly asleep only to wake in the dark hours with her grandfather's voice singing one of his favourite songs by Rod Stewart into her mind. Sailing.

He sang of being home, of crossing seas to be near his beloved, and flying like a bird to be with her.

Grace marvelled. She hadn't heard her grandfather's voice in over nineteen years.

Such solace Grace felt to know her grandparents were reuniting.

Then dosing back to sleep she was given a dream. Another gift.

She walked through a door into a white room that had a table and booth chairs around it, and another door at the far end of the table, to Grace's right. Agnes was sitting opposite that door, to Grace's left as she walked in. Her grandmother motioned for Grace to sit beside her. The younger woman felt the surrealness of the situation as she sat on the booth next to her grandmother. Grace took her hand and could feel her smooth, soft skin and smell her familiar scent. Her heart expanded.

'What are you doing here?' She asked.

Grace's dreaming self was aware her grandmother had passed that day.

'I just came to tell you I'm okay Tiny.'

Agnes smiled the most peace filled smile. Love flowed from her into Grace. Then she got up as the door opposite them opened. Bright light shone within the room, billowing into the space. Grace could see the outline of another person in the doorway. Her grandmother walked to the door and Grace hurriedly rose to follow her.

As Agnes stepped across the threshold, she turned, saying, 'Not yet Tiny, not yet.'

Grace was not permitted to follow her grandmother into the light. The door, seemingly of its own accord, closed behind Agnes, leaving Grace to exit the way she had entered.

Grace woke up giving thanks to the ministry that permitted the dream that was not a dream, but a precious reassurance. She thanked God for the word and the chance to see her darling grandma again.

When Grace awoke it was strange for her to be in a world without her grandmother. Only after Agnes passed did Grace realise that she had known her grandmother's presence all her life. No matter where they were in the world, there was a connection between them that permitted Grace to feel her grandma. The day after Agnes died that connection was broken. It did return sometime later, but for a while it was gone. Agnes was no longer in the world, and Grace could no longer feel her presence. She described it to her friends as the most peculiar thing; as if she could no longer feel a part of her body that had gone numb. It just was no longer there.

Many a time Grace and Agnes had talked about what it would be like after death. While she had been brought up Christian, Church of Scotland every day and twice on Sundays in Peterhead, Agnes and Donald did not continue church attendance once married.

Agnes found it difficult to reconcile a loving God with the horrors of war, having nursed the bodies of broken men, and the stories she knew about her husband's treatment in the prisoner of war camp.

'Do you believe in God, grandma?' Grace asked on one of their hot chips by the sea outings.

'Oh yes,' she said. 'But not the Church way so much anymore.'

'What about eternal life? What do you think happens to you when you go?'

'Well,' said Agnes, 'everything is energy. We are energy, and energy can't die. So yes, I think we continue in one way or another.'

That satisfied her granddaughter who didn't like to think of an afterlife without her grandmother in it. There and then Grace made Agnes agree that whoever went first, they would let the other one know they were all right. The signal that they had was to blow in the ear. If Agnes went first she would blow in Grace's ear. And if Grace died first, she would do the same with her grandmother. Well, they chuckled, laughing at the thought of whoever it was brushing away an annoying breeze that kept bothering them, making loud whooshes in the ear.

The day Agnes passed, Grace had comfort from the gift of the dream with her grandmother telling her she was okay, but she already missed her grandma's presence in the world.

Grace had to move. She couldn't sit in the hotel room with her thoughts and the grief that was upon her. She'd spoken with her mum and dad, and they'd cried together. She'd shared messages with the twins and with her uncle Jim, but it was all a bit unreal. That afternoon, Grace wrote a poem for the funeral that her brother David would read out. Then she booked a train ticket out of Manchester.

Grace had looked online and discovered Saint Winefride's Well in Holywell, in the north of Wales. Her grandmother's name was Agnes Winifred MacMillan and she was fond of Winifred. This well in Wales was known to have healing properties and to cause miraculous cures, with reports of healing since the early medieval years. It became associated with Saint Winefride, who was beheaded by a local prince, Caradoc, after she refused his romantic advances. It is said that she was fleeing to the church her uncle, Saint Beuno built when Caradoc caught up to her. On the spot where Winefride's head fell, a spring came up through the ground, enabling Saint Beuno to restore her to life.

Beuno came out from the church where he took up his niece's head and placed it back on her body. He then prayed and she was raised to life. A white scar encircled her neck thereafter, witness to her martyrdom. While her relics were held in Shrewsbury Cathedral, the well had been a pilgrimage site consistently for over thirteen centuries.

Grace smiled to think that only two years earlier she and her mum had visited Shrewsbury Cathedral in honour of Agnes. Her grandmother had been delighted.

Now, three days after Agnes' passing, Grace entered the

Sanctuary of the Well, with its Crypt, outer pool and small chapel. She paid her respects to Saint Winefride, and took some time in prayer for her grandmother. Visitors who had been in the chapel and surrounds went on their way leaving Grace alone in the Sanctuary.

After quietly speaking about her grandma and her passing to the saint, and thanking her for the healing miracles over the centuries, Grace stepped outside again to the outer pool. There, she knelt down and washed her hands and arms in the spring water. Grace didn't know what to expect, if anything, but as she sat there by the pool, the cool water glistening on her skin in the late morning sun, Grace felt the most radiant peace come upon her. Forgetfulness born of God's grace illumined life and love and joy where moments earlier grief and anguish had reigned. Peace so soft, altogether soothing, touched her body and rested her mind.

Grace sat there a while by the well, and collected a sample of the water with bottles provided in the adjacent shop to take with her. In silence, she left the pilgrimage site and rather than return to her Snowdonia mountainside B and B, Grace drove further west onto the island of Anglesey.

It was an unusually warm day for that time of year in Britain and she headed towards the western coastline and beaches. As she drove along, Grace suddenly felt compelled to stop the car at the point where a large ridge of sand dunes could be seen either side of the road. She thought this rather unusual that suddenly green pasturelands should give way to what appeared to be beach sands either side of the main road.

Having parked the car, she noticed that a monument board had been erected nearby, and a gate led into the dunes. Passing by the tourist notice without reading it, she walked through the gate onto the sand on the left side of the road. Grace was fascinated. Out of nowhere, green pastures, cows and sheep, had given way to these rises of sand dunes. She walked and walked and walked, not really knowing why. It was as if the dunes were calling her. Eventually, Grace came to what must have been a waterway at some point. There, God showed her villagers washing their clothes and bodies, babies in hand, children running around. At some point in history a community of people lived alongside this waterway. Now it was empty of life, akin to a desert landscape. Grace marvelled at the press of time upon the place and how transient the life of civilisation, in all its forms, is in the face of time and space.

As she was pondering this, Grace realised she had broken Australia's cardinal rule for travelling. She had not brought water with her on her walk and in the heat of the day, she was now quite parched. Turning back to the car, she noticed the beating sun at its zenith. Her pulse started to pound outside of her body. It took concentration to slow her breathing even as she picked up the pace, making a direct line towards the road.

Less than twenty metres from her car and the promise of a cool drink, a wind rose up about the woman. Out of nowhere, sand began to stir and swirl around her. Though there was no breeze, in the proximity nearest her, a small whirlwind of air and sand spun around her. And amidst the whoosh of the air, there it came… the distinct feeling of her grandma. In that very moment, Grace knew that God was granting she and her grandmother their promise to one another.

Grace felt the familiar warmth in her heart of Agnes' presence, which had been absent three days since her passing. As she noticed this, a clear and focused blowing of air cut through the swirling wind and was directed into Grace's right ear.

Her grandmother blew in her ear. She was alive. And God had helped her fulfil her promise to Grace. And then she was gone again. But Grace's faith in eternal life was upheld there and then.

It was one thing to have been comforted in dream by her grandmother. Grace had experienced a number of gifts of God, including the prophetic in dream. But to have the Holy Spirit manipulate the physical world with such a sign of wonder, Grace was grateful and believing beyond doubt. Smiling broadly, all thought of her thirst gone from mind, quenched entirely in spirit, Grace glanced at the notice board beside the entrance gate. It gave the story of a community of ancient peoples who had lived along a riverbed that had long ago dried up.

Grace laughed out loud. Looking heavenward, she declared, 'Thank you. Thank you.'

Sparing a thought for Saint Winefride, Grace smiled broadly with gratitude.

'A healing miracle, indeed,' she said aloud.

And Grace's faith in the intercessory power of the Saints

remained a living truth ever after.

Sitting in her car, which would not start, the radio beeped. The window wipers flickered. The horn tooted and the door locks opened and shut of their own accord. Grace simply sat still. Whatever power the Holy Spirit had exerted to bring about this gift from God had lingering effects in the material world. A moment later everything worked fine.

This experience was the first time Grace personally had recourse to believe that life continued after death. Without doubt, she knew that God had permitted her to experience the ongoing life of her beloved grandmother, first in dream, and then alongside those ancient sand dunes.

Grace remained in Wales for the week. She missed her grandma's funeral, but was able to watch the recording. Grace knew that if she was to experience the heavenly reality of her grandma's ongoing life, she needed to be set apart from the loss. She couldn't go back for the funeral, amidst the family grief and worldly busyness. She was aware that spiritual realities are best discerned away from everyday affairs. And while a part of Grace wanted to share in the family's gathering for their beloved mother and grandmother, and to be there for her mum, the greater part of Grace needed to be available to the heavenly gifts that testified to Agnes' eternal life. And now she felt so blessed to have stayed and to have had that confirmation. Her grandma lived on, and Grace could witness that truth to her family.

Leaving Britain, Grace flew into Adelaide before Melbourne to be with her family. Together, they gathered to take Agnes and Donald's ashes down to Moana Beach. They would be released into the sea they came to enjoy so much. Grace had the privilege of leading the family in prayers and the scattering of the ashes as they scattered the remains of their mortal bodies into the waters. It was a special moment, celebrating their life while holding them both dear in heart.

Donald and Agnes would have approved mightily, particularly when a great wave and wind came up and knocked a few of the family over, blowing a good portion of their ashes back onto them. There were laughs all around. Grace could just imagine her grandparents having a good chuckle.

As she looked back upon these last experiences with her grandmother, Grace perceived them as a mercy ministry. An act of holy grace had watered the seed already planted by God in her soul to abide in Jesus. Grace knew God had orchestrated heavenly blessings for her to be comforted in her grief.

And, as Grace heeded divine leadings, and as her Christian walk deepened, she learnt that in the depths of every soul there is someone each person is meant to find. And, there is a place of home where every one is called to be. Grace learnt that in order to live and have her being with God, and to come home to God's heavenly place, she, like all of God's children must become the flowering fruit of the seed of God that God has planted in humanity. Only then can a human destiny be fulfilled. Only then can a person walk out of the shadow of death and live the joy filled plan God has for them: a plan that raises a person up to be more and more in God's likeness; a plan that prospers, that does not harm but gives hope and a future; a plan to see each individual live in and with God today, tomorrow and into eternal life.

Having come to know all this, Grace was now ready to respond to the word she'd received about moving for her work with God.

'Yes. Yes, your will God is my will.'

And as soon as she said yes, the way was opened for her. She was accepted into the British Interfaith Seminary.

Without a job to go to and no plan other than the one she knew God had for her, Grace wrapped up her life in Melbourne. She resigned from her counselling job, sold her car and gave her furniture to charity. Then, on the 16th of October 2012, our darling, now forty-four years old, said goodbye to family and friends, and to the country that had raised her.

And a chorus of heavenly hosts chimed, *This is the Lord's doing; it is marvellous in our eyes. This is the day that the Lord has made; let us rejoice and be glad in it.*

As the plane soared skyward, and tears gently surrendered, Grace felt her heart unfurl and her spine tingle as her countenance ignited in spiritual joy. She could feel the providential wings of God's promises inexorably drawing her forward. And somewhere in the recesses of her consciousness, little Grace confidently strode out beyond the boundary of her grandparents' home. Answering the divine call, walking hand in hand with God, Grace's suitcase was now filled with a wellspring of new faith.

# 28

# Answering the Divine Call

O *habibi*, darling, you have witnessed the unfolding of Grace's journey in answer to the divine call. She has taken you into the fallen nature of humanity and risen to the sound of angels trumpeting, 'Hallelujah!'

What a spiritual triumph. What a testimony to the heavenly workings that aid in the alignment of a person to the soul of God's making. A whirlwind of tragedy and drama, of failings, and undertakings sublime. My, my.

In Grace's footsteps, you see the pursuit of love and the transformative power of trust in the face of divine love. Through her struggles and triumphs, you understand that the journey of answering the divine call is not without its challenges, that the divine call is not a promise of a trouble-free life but an assurance of divine presence amidst the struggles. You observe through Grace's walk that a person is refined when responding to God.

And that it is in response to the divine call that your soul becomes free of worldly entanglement as your heart is purified. For within those challenges lie the seeds of growth, redemption, restoration and the offer of a profound union with God.

Yes, Grace's story beckons you to reflect on your own spiritual journey, urging you to embrace authenticity and to shed the burdens imposed by the world and by yourself. Her story serves as a beacon of hope, demonstrating the resilience of the human spirit and its capacity to conquer worldly limitations by accepting God's call, and the steadfast ministry of Jesus Christ.

Throughout Grace's journey, Jesus' presence is a constant, calling her to him, and gently guiding her—and you—through life's ebbs and flows. Even in her doubts and rejections, God's tender love heals and transforms her. You see how Jesus' faithful companionship offers solace and hope, reminding you that in your own journey, he walks beside you, weaving his presence into every chapter of your life.

These are early steps for Grace in her deification journey. In this first chapter of her spiritual awakening, you see how Grace draws on what is available to her. She does not yet know how to call on Christ and the Holy Spirit for healing or understand the gift of God's grace in her life, but she responds to the love and desire within her for spiritual truth.

You will have noticed too that God's grace is extended to our darling Grace through the divine embrace, the vision and guidance of Blessed Mary, the intercession of the angel, Raphael, and the holy visitation of Jesus Christ, calling her to himself, while Grace was yet a lay person, and unbaptised. This upholds the words of the Eastern Orthodox Fathers that the Lord does not discriminate in his call upon humanity. All persons are called. Always.

And while God's grace is evident in these of God's pursuits of Grace, it is her response that illuminates God's gift to Grace. That response is at this stage in Grace's spiritual growth marked by her growing faith and repentance. It signals a shift towards a gospel-centred life. For as the Apostle Peter declares, the divine call is a journey of transformation and holiness, aligning each person with the image of Christ: *As he who called you is holy, be holy yourselves in all your conduct, for it is written, 'You shall be holy, for I am holy'.*

The evidence of this holiness growing lies not so much in the mystical phenomena Grace experiences but in her repentance—for life confession, and for what will later become a life of confession towards spiritual purification. Repentance is a significant sign of transformation towards holiness. The divine call evokes in a person a yearning for goodness and for righteousness, to be right with God. This too is given by God's grace, and it stimulates inner transformation through the work of the Holy Spirit, conforming individuals to the image of Christ.

Glory, glory, these most holy blessings of faith and repentance are what you witness in the beginnings of Grace's spiritual growth, and they are, if you choose to look, the strengthening fibre behind values that have grown you and which are evident today in your own life. And it is through these most glorious of virtues that a sincere and intimate dialogue opens up between you and God. God 'out there' becomes God right here, someone so close, so personal, so breathtakingly present as to reach for and touch. This is but one gift of the Spirit of God, your most loyal and faithful friend who is calling you to the purpose God has for you, glorifying God and you, as you make your way home.

You see then in this story an invitation to not only embrace God's guidance, to listen to the whispers of your soul, and to trust in the unseen hand leading you, but to enter into the currents of pruning and divine shaping that make you, by grace, more holy. Within this you are reminded of the opportunity each person has towards eternal splendour in the deification path God has laid out for you towards everlasting life.

Well, *Habibi*, darling, as you anticipate the next chapter in Grace's life, *Living Faith*, may you be inspired to embark upon your own spiritual odyssey with God or deepen the intimacy of personal connection you already have with God.

Having cried out to God, 'Yes! Yes! Your will is my will,' now reach for the divine love that transcends all earthly expectations. Discover in depth the heavenly ministry that abounds ready to uphold your spiritual unfoldment. Make way for the life-altering power of spiritual truth as you draw nearer to the Spirit of God that lives within you. This invitation really is a dynamic heavenly motion that beckons you to take one step after another, hand in hand with God as you consistently and dedicatedly turn around in faith to answer the divine call.

✣

*The adventure continues…*

# Book 2

## GRACE Living Faith

Venture into the heart of unfolding destiny with the second book in the Grace trilogy, *Living Faith.* Journey alongside Grace now, as she heeds the divine call to live resolutely available to God's promises and plan upon her life.

In this captivating testimony, Grace learns what it means to live by faith as she encounters worldly opportunities, moments of doubt and profound heavenly leadings.

Steeped in the power of the Holy Spirit, Grace enters into a healing ministry that sets the tone for her life in Britain. As she navigates her way through Celtic landscapes and traditions, obstructions to God's will in her life are peeled away. Then, just when Grace's purpose seems clear, a breathtaking revelation emerges, one that promises to redefine her life and the reality of the reader's own spiritual quest and formation.

*Living Faith* is more than one woman's story; it is a testament to the supernatural reality of faith and God's gifts for a person. This narrative will enchant, inspire, and challenge you, reminding you of the profound wisdom that comes with true faith as you live the divine call. It provides the reader with new understanding about promises waiting to be unveiled in your own life while revealing spiritual practices that support living faith towards union with God.

GRACE
Living Faith
BOOK 2
A WOMAN OF GOD

Printed in Great Britain
by Amazon

34022791R00155